ADOLESCENCE AND CHARACTER DISTURBANCE

James B. McCarthy, Ph.D.

UNIVERSITY
PRESS OF
AMERICA

Lanham • New York • London

Copyright © 1995 by
University Press of America,® Inc.
4720 Boston Way
Lanham, Maryland 20706

3 Henrietta Street
London WC2E 8LU England

Library of Congress Cataloging-in-Publication Data

McCarthy, James B.
Adolescence and character disturbance / James B. McCarthy.
p.   cm.
Includes bibliographical references and index.
1. Personality disorders in adolescence.   2. Personality in
adolescence.   3. Personality development.   4. Anxiety in
adolescence.   5. Adolescent analysis.   I. Title.
RJ506.P32M33   1994
616.85'8'0835—dc20   94–16770 CIP

ISBN 0–8191–9582–0 (cloth : alk. paper)
ISBN 0–8191–9583–9 (pbk. : alk. paper)

 The paper used in this publication meets the minimum requirements of
American National Standard for Information Sciences—Permanence
of Paper for Printed Library Materials, ANSI Z39.48–1984.

FOR JOAN McCARTHY,

with my gratitude and admiration

CONTENTS

PREFACE

He tried to build a breakwater of order and elegance against the sordid tide of life without him and to dam up, by rules of conduct and active interests and new filial relations, the powerful recurrence of tides within him.

James Joyce

Heraclitus believed that character was destiny. For Rosseau, the period of adolescence suggested romantic possibilities for the awakening of rationality and the attainment of full harmony with human nature. Since antiquity, philosophers and writers have sought a clear vision of how innate processes and external circumstances allow the maturing adolescent to fully inhabit the characteristics of the personality. However, psychoanalytic theorists have provided the most profound understanding of both character formation and character reorganization during adolescence. Freud's papers on character types, his ideas about the anal character, and his writings on adolescence, all offered prototypical standards for the in-depth assessment of the evolution and consolidation of character. This volume contracts and synthesizes concepts from classical Freudian theory, interpersonal psychoanalysis and British object relations theories which have illuminated these issues. Its format combines aspects of an historical survey of theories of adolescence and character disturbance, with clinical chapters on the role of primitive anxieties in shaping character trends.

My main subjects are the jolting dynamics of primitive anxiety states and a comparison of the psychoanalytic models of character reorganization during adolescence. The approach I have chosen to these themes does not include innovations in developmental and psychoanalytic contructs. My intent is to offer clinicians and students a glimpse of the New York University Postdoctoral Program's spirit of openness to the complexity and diversity of psychoanalytic thought. My dual focus on primitive anxiety states and adolescent character trends stems from a simple thesis. The adolescent maturational process of individuation frominternal objects is analagous to the adult analysand's unconscious resolution of the terror of growth and change.

The outline of psychoanalytic character typology has evolved from the 1900's emphasis on instincts and libido and the 1930's emphasis on ego processes, to our present day concern with the supraordinate concept of the self. In the history of psychoanalytic theory, the concept of character has represented a controversial abstraction and a specific term for the structure and functioning of the personality. According to each psychoanalytic theoretical model, character is allied with the concept of identity, and it forms the basis for both relatedness and psychopathology. During adolescence, character increasingly refers to the relatively fixed aspects of the personality which organize the internal world as well as the external world of interpersonal relationships.

ACKNOWLEDGEMENTS

A number of people have given me much encouragement and support over a period of years which have culminated in this work. I want to express my deep appreciation to Drs. Louis C. English, Serge E. Hadjolian, Jerilyn Kronen, Marylou J. Lionells, and John R. Ozehosky. Many colleagues have helped me with the progression of my ideas, and I am especially grateful to Drs. Harold B. Davis, Gladys Branley Guarton, Susan Mulliken, and David Webb for their thoughtful reading of many chapters. I would also like to thank Mrs. Michelle Cruz for her patient, diligent preparation of this manuscript. In addition, I want to thank my patients for their role in the facilitation of my own growth.

My understanding of the clinical data which will be discussed has evolved over twenty years of private practice and supervisory work. Much earlier, shorter versions of a number of chapters have appeared as papers in journals whose editors I would like to thank for their permission to include the material. Chapters Three, Four, Six and Eight are based on papers which were published in the *American Journal of Psychoanalysis:* "Abusive Families and Character Formation", 1990, 50, 181-186, "Psychoanalytic Psychotherapy and the Fear of Death" 1981, 41, 21-30, "Resistance and Countertransference in Child and Adolescent Psychotherapy", 1989, 49, 67-76; and "Narcissism and the Self in Homicidal Adolescents", 1978, 38, 19-31. An abbreviated form of Chapter Five appeared in the *Journal of the American Academy of Psychoanalysis*, "Resistance and Primitive Anxiety", 1985, 13, 181-189. Chapter Seven consists of a blend of two papers, "Paranoia and Omnipotent Symbiosis in Borderline Adolescents" and a much earlier paper which was published in *Modern Psychoanalysis*, "Infantile Narcissism: A study of Symbiosis and Aggression in Borderline Children", 1979, 4, 71-81. A form of chapter Nine previously appeared in *Issues in Ego Psychology*, "Locomotion and Adolescent Identity Loss", 1984, 1, 4-10.

PART I

CHARACTER FORMATION

CHAPTER ONE

Character: An Introduction

... The various classical psychopathological conditions represented, not fixations at specific libidinal phases, but specific techniques for regulating relationships with internal objects...

W. Ronald Fairbairn

A twenty nine year old man who suffered from chronic depressed moods of boredom and emptiness reported a dream to his analyst.

> The patient was affectionately playing with a kitten in a barren hotel room in the dream when he sensed the nearly menacing presence of a tiger. At the point of this realization, he became absolutely frantic in his efforts to remove the kitten from the room. The associations to the dream suggested intense anxiety superimposed upon a literal terror of being devoured and dismembered.

Should the patient's depressive character traits be understood as the result of castration anxiety and Oedipal punishment or as the pre-Oedipal terror of emotional contact with a devouring murderous internalized parent? Was this man suggesting that his depression was first recreated in the analytic relationship by his insatiable needs to be fed and rescued, and then perpetuated by his unacknowledged self devaluations and self attacks? Did the dream also imply that the patient would be destroyed if his dysphoric moods of gloom gave way to lasting moments of happiness and spontaneity? Could he not tolerate either other's warmth, or instances of his own giving to himself because they would mean that the insides of his body might be emptied and eaten as he had dreaded in the first years of his life? Had the analyst's unrecognized countertransference responses precipitated exchanges in which the patient a statement of potential insight about how the patient toyed with people much as he had been treated in a ferociously hostile family environment? All of these formulations of the material presented valid, clinically meaningful questions about the patient's depressive character trends.

The diverse expression of this patient's characterological tendencies pointed to the controversy in psychoanalytic theory concerning the nature of character organization and character change. William James wrote that recesses of feeling fall in the blind strata of character where individuality lies. The individuality of character has been accounted for by some psychoanalytic theorists as a derivation of drives and internal structures. Other theorists have knitted together a concept of character as either an organizing principle or a manifestation of ties to internalized objects. Character traits have been considered not only representations of inner states, but also expressions of defenses and developmental deficits. They are simultaneously comprised of symbolic representations of both experiential data and internalized relationships which are played out in interpersonal transactions. During adolescence, characterological tendencies are consolidated in a relatively fixed direction. As the adolescent's individuation from the family proceeds, and as cognitive maturation continues, object relational patterns become more stable. They are increasingly interwoven with the adolescent's evolving resolution of neurotic and developmental conflicts. The adolescent's relatedness, defenses, cognition and affect all take on at least a distinct pattern, if not clear signs of psychopathology. The paranoid adolescent, for example, seeks out and unwittingly provokes threatening encounters which reinforce grandiosity and suspiciousness. The nature of character consolidation and the issue of how to facilitate character change during adolescence have constituted long-standing challenges to psychoanalytic theory and practice. However, there has been no uniform comprehensive psychoanalytic theory of character.

The classical Freudian, object relations and interpersonal psychoanalytic models of character have each assigned a distinct hierarchical status to the importance of fantasy in character formation. Each model's clinical theory has implied dissimilar views of anxiety and transference as the arenas for character change. Different outlooks on resistance, transference and countertransference, which are implicit in the metapsychologies of character, have suggested different emphases for psychoanalytic work. Classical Freudian theorists have described character formation through drive defenses and structural deficits. Object relations theorists have depicted character in terms of defensive positions against the dangers of internalized object relations. Interpersonal psychoanalytic theorists have stressed a view of character as the inner organization of experience which governs our grasp of meaning and use of symbolic processes. All three psychoanalytic theoretical models have highlighted the significance of primitive anxiety and trauma in character formation. They have differed widely about the nature of symbolism and what it is that character symbolizes. As an integrative summary of the interpersonal and object relations perspectives, my own view has been that character consists of a synthesis of the organization of experience and the template of the world of internal objects. The reworking of this synthesis during adolescence will be elaborated in a number of the following chapters on primitive anxiety and personality disturbance.

Despite the immediacy of new experience, character remains the home to which the self inevitably returns. The English word, character, derives from Greek roots which mean to engrave or to furrow with distinctive qualities. The term, character, therefore ordinarily signifies the weaving of a pattern. By late adolescence, a pattern emerges of enduring defensive trends, internalized relationships, and self images which define one as a person. A primary aim of this work will be to contrast classical Freudian, object relations and interpersonal psychoanalytic views of character and their elucidations of character disturbance in adolescence. In order to accomplish this aim, I will first compare these three psychoanalytic models in terms of not only their concepts of anxiety and primitive anxiety, but also their approaches to the goals of the psychoanalytic encounter. My secondary purpose will be to sketch characterological deficits during adolescence, such as those which distinguish homicidal adolescents and borderline adolescents, as well as those who experience identity loss. A third principal objective will be to explore adolescents' orchestration of primitive anxiety during both character consolidation and the psychoanalytic process. After a discussion of the concept of primitive anxiety, this initial chapter will survey the history of psychoanalytic theory in order to compare models of character formation and the goals of analytic practice.

Primitive Anxiety and Adolescence

Once Sigmund Freud (1915, 1923) abandoned the seduction theory of neurosis, he designated the concept of signal anxiety as the corner-stone of the ego's operations and character formation. Signal anxiety amounted to the ego's reactions to instinctual danger and remembered trauma. At that point in the evolution of Freudian theory, the nature of what was repressed changed from memories of incestuous seductions to libidinal conflicts about the expression of sexual and aggressive drives. From that historical foundation, different notions of anxiety have distinguished the Freudian, interpersonal and object relations models of character. For Harry Stack Sullivan, anxiety was communicated by empathy, and it was universally interpersonal in its origins. Because of anxiety, what was dissociated in character or, according to Sullivan's terminology, the self system, was not merely unconscious conflict. Anything which was unacceptable to the self system, that is, anything which met with the threat of disapproval, could be dissociated. Even one's greatest assets and healthiest tendencies could therefore be dissociated. For object relations theorists, anxiety necessarily arose out of conflicts with internalized objects, and it did not simply develop because of drive conflicts. For many object relations theorists, especially Melanie Klein and Donald Winnicott, primitive anxieties and Oedipal anxieties were fully present in definitive form in the first year of life. Even the most seemingly unrelated states of schizoid detachment were always object relational within this theoretical model. Not much of a distinction has been made in object relations theories between neurotic character traits and psychotic disorders since character traits were conceptualized as universal defensive expressions of psychotic anxiety.

Psychoanalytic theorists of different orientations have explored primitive anxiety's disruption of inner continuity. This discontinuity ranges from the preverbal terrors of the dissolution of the body and the self to a more differentiated fear of death in the better integrated person. The separation processes inherent in adolescent development add to the adolescent's vulnerability to primitive anxiety. In states of primitive anxiety, separation fears are confounded by the equation of the loss of the object with the disintegration of the self (Khan, 1963). Adolescents' primitive anxieties may be manifest as preverbal fears of disintegration or as more articulated fears of annihilation of the self and the internal object.

According to Freudian theory, the ego provided defenses against the full spectrum of instinctual dangers. Trauma served as an organizing principle which structured the levels of anxiety (Greenacre, 1967). Neurotic anxiety took the form of fear of guilt or fear of the superego. Nearness to psychotic anxiety involved dissociated, fragmentary states which included: the fear of the ego's submergence into the id (A. Freud, 1936), the fear of falling, infinitely, (Winnicott, 1958), the fear of the loss of body boundaries (Mahler, 1976), and the fear of being emptied of an internal fluid which constitutes the body self (P. Kernberg, 1980). Melanie Klein and Harry Stack Sullivan first attached great significance to the term, primitive anxiety, and they each described its profound influence on the evolution of the personality. Although some of their ideas were developed around the same period in the 1930's and 1940's, they wrote from completely alien theoretical points of view. Both Klein and Sullivan considered primitive anxiety as crucial to their understands of psychopathology. For Klein (1932), the origins of primitive anxiety were explained by the infant's innate destructiveness and by the vicissitudes of the death instinct during the first few months of life. In Kleinian theory, the death instinct was automatically projected onto the breast, and the child's fear of death stemmed from its own aggression and greed. Sullivan (1953) illuminated the influence of, what he called, not-me experience. Not-me experience was equivalent to the felt experience of primitive anxiety, such as during adolescence, when, he suggested, the young person is governed by the struggle to avoid emptiness and the pain of interpersonal isolation. Sullivan's (1940, 1956) writings on primitive anxiety took into account the phenomenology of the anxiety which is present in nightmares and in schizophrenia. From the interpersonal and relational points of view, the feared loss of self in primitive anxiety reflected a neurotic lack of differentiation and an intolerance for the anxiety which is necessary in maintaining separateness.

For the British object relations theorists and the interpersonal theorists, primitive anxiety also recaptured the agonies of early trauma in the family. Winnicott (1975) suggested that primitive anxiety was present in the infant's response to insufficient maternal care. Primitive anxiety was given final assuagement, according to Winnicott (1974), in the fear of a breakdown which masks a breakdown that actually did occur in early life. Little (1981) noted that primitive anxieties dominate transference reactions in borderline conditions, and that for individuals with borderline personality organization, acting out can be seen as the activation of a memory of the child's toxic environment. For the object relations theorist W.R. Fairbairn (1952), states of primitive anxiety evolved as a consequence of disruptions of early dependence. These disruptions, which resulted in the divorce of mental life from the life of feeling, occurred in, what Fairbairn termed, schizoid anxiety.

Sullivan's (1953) point-that adolescents show a susceptibility to primitive anxiety-has been corroborated by both clinical and research investigations of anxieties about death.   The deemphasis on psychic structure and the emphasis on experience in his theory sounded a note of hopefulness about the ameliorative effect of adolescence on trauma. Sullivan's developmental theory shared little common ground with the assumption that the earlier the trauma, the worse the outcome and the greater the psychopathology.

Psychoanalytic work with adult patients often chronicles the impact of adolescent development on the following areas which will be expanded later.   Although character is not completely delineated during adolescence,   by   late   adolescence   compromise   strategies   and identifications with internal objects have been fully established. During adolescence leaps in cognitive maturation enhance symbolic processes which contain integrations of self images and integrations of thought and affect. Greater abstraction ability makes it possible for the adolescent to engage in introspection and to make more effective use of complex symbols.   Adolescents'   imagery   and   dream   symbolism   reflects characterological tendencies, such as grandiosity or anxiety about inner reflection, which inhibit identity synthesis. Adolescents' confusion and ambivalence about individuation adds to their familiarity with primitive anxiety and death anxiety. Finally, adolescents' struggles with sexuality and identity experimentation take place with considerable readjustments of self-esteem. What A. Reich (1962, 1973) had earlier depicted as the ego's efforts to maintain self-esteem regulation, Kohut (1971, 1977) described as part of his theory of the transformation of the selfobject. Kohut's theory of personality development maintained an object relations perspective, and I will refer to some of his ideas in my discussion of homicidal adolescents and narcissistic adolescents.   Kohut's followers have characterized the main task of adolescence as the enhancement of empathy for oneself via the transformation of the selfobject (Wolf, 1982). Character formation came about in Blos's (1968) Freudian developmental theory as the result of the "incomplete passage" through adolescence. The developmental task of adolescence, for Blos (1979), has been to achieve the transition between character traits and character formation. This transition takes place as changes in ego and drive organization engender the creation of a formal character. The sweep of these theories of adolescence and primitive anxiety encompasses cognitive, structural and object relations changes during the adolescent period. The breadth of such changes clearly extends beyond what was originally considered in classical psychoanalytic theory to be the *sine qua non* of adolescence, namely the recapitulation and resolution of the Oedipus Complex.

Freudian Theories of Character

In combining the economic and structural models of the mind, Freud wrote that the limits of character were determined by the level of libidinal fixation. He left it to the early Freudians, chiefly Abraham, Reich, and later, Fenichel to codify a complete definition of character as a theory of mental structure and defensive operations which emphasized the ego (Lax, 1989). Freud (1906) traced specific defenses in each of the psychosexual stages which worked to accomplish repression of the infantile neurosis. He described the oral character, the phallic character, and in his widely known 1908 paper, the eroticism of the anal character. Freud (1908) explained in this paper that the character traits of orderliness, obstinacy and parsimoniousness were unconscious extensions of anal eroticism. The symbolism of libidinal fixation in the anal retentive and anal aggressive phases paralleled Abraham's (1924, 1925) later accounts of the oral receptive, oral aggressive, and genital character traits. Another of the earliest classifications of character types was Freud's (1914) delineation of the psychoneurosis and the narcissistic neuroses, by which he meant, the psychoses and the severe character disorders. The latter group, he felt, were incapable of forming the transference neurosis and therefore could not be successfully treated by the psychoanalytic method. Freud's paper *Inhibitions, Symptoms and Anxiety,* which was published in 1926, examined the psychodynamic ties of character traits to the types of resistance. This theme was expanded more fully in many of the early Freudian writings on psychoanalytic techniques, especially those by Reich and Fenichel.

According to Freud's later work, character symptoms and character traits arose in order to remove the ego from danger. Anna Freud (1936) added the principle that particular defenses, which characterized each neurosis, occurred in states of fixation in neurotic symptoms. Character organization, which was a more general concept in classical Freudian theory, became the final product of the ego's synthesis of conflicts, defenses and drives.

In classical psychoanalytic theory, the patterning of character referred not only to the organization of psychic conflict, but also to the accommodations which occur between defenses and drives or wishes and memories. The emphasis in this early Freudian model was placed on affects and defenses in relation to conflicts (Jones, 1929; Alexander, 1933). Repression, sublimation and reaction formation-the defenses of the Oedipal era-hence became the main defensive components of the neurotic character.   Fenichel (1945) foresaw in *The Psychoanalytic Theory of Neurosis* that habitual ego attitudes can become character traits. Both develop, he proposed, much like defenses in order to be applied over and over again in order to ward off instinctual danger.   Fenichel (1953) formalized the Freudian view of character traits as compromise accommodations between ego defenses and instinctual drives. Perhaps the most widely known early classical Freudian investigation of this subject was W. Reich's *Character Analysis* which first appeared in 1933. This book dexterously went beyond drive theory. For Reich, character proclaimed the ego's armature. Reich advocated the direct confrontation of resistances and bringing them to the patient's awareness.   He implicated patients' overall attitudes and general modes of relating to the analyst as repressed characterological tendencies which formed resistances.   His approach infused classical Freudian technique with militaristic metaphors in which the analyst does battle with resistances, and it underscored the rigidity of character resistances.

The ego psychologists Hartmann and Erikson emphasized both structural deficits and the ego's ways of dealing with the world as crucial to character.   The Freudian model of character was further codified in the 1950's and the 1960's by many classical theorists. Greenson (1967) believed that character consists of the ego's organization in dealing with the demands of the id and the superego, together with its habitual methods of coping with both internal and external demands. Beginning with Freud's discussion of the superego and his papers on character, object relations were included in the original formulations of character. In *Mourning and Melancholia* (1917) Freud demonstrated the importance of identification with internalized objects, and he later embellished this theme in *The Ego and the Id (1923)*. However, object relations were not given foremost significance in Freud's writings.   Although Freud measured the developmental course of object libido, which he distinguished from ego libido, the focus in his case studies and papers on character was clearly on psychosexual fixations and concomitant defensive styles.

Object Relations Theories of Character

The object relations theories of character espoused by Winnicott, Guntrip and Fairbairn were derived from the influence of Melanie Klein. Klein (1948) was convinced that personality was formed as a result of the infant's innate envy and destructiveness during the first year when object images are distinguished from self images.   Other object relations theorists who were more Freudian, such as Jacobson (1964), have assessed the formation of self images and object images in terms of developmental changes in psychic structure.   Klein's emphasis on the primitive defenses of splitting and projection, also during the infant's first year, has been taken up by many theorists of character.   Her concepts of projective identification and splitting have become a mainstay of object relations theorists' conceptualization of the borderline personality. Klein's view of character was based on the primary significance of the infant's unconscious fantasies and anxieties.   In her theory, relatively little attention was paid to the reality of the child's life in the family, since personality was thought to be largely determined by the ego's permanent fantasies (Segal, 1964).   From the time of Klein's introduction to the British Psychoanalytic Society in 1926, her extensions of Freud's writings on object relations provided an enormous contribution to the psychoanalytic models of character formation.

As one of the most influential object relations theorists, Fairbairn suggested that Klein did not go far enough in stressing the centrality of the schizoid position and the depressive position.   According to Fairbairn's (1941) object relations theory of personality, character was determined by the strength of relational patterns during the first year of life.   Character traits were always to be understood for Fairbairn as object ties. In Fairbairn's carefully constructed theory, the object was always the goal of libido.   Character traits were formed by the difficulties of the ego in making contact with an object. In agreement with Winnicott's notion that the ego began as a primary relatedness, Fairbairn (1941) argued that the investigation of psychopathology consisted of the study of the ego's relationship with internalized objects. Primary character types were determined as being a function of either schizoid or depressive states. Fairbairn (1952) affirmed that obsessional, phobic and hysterical tendencies were variations of flight from, acceptance of, or rejection of the internal object ties. This emphasis on defensive postures in relation to internal objects was reiterated from a neoFreudian vantagepoint in Karen Horney's rendering of character as composites of movement toward, against and away from people.

For Fairbairn, the intensity of the fixation in early object ties was always the essential factor in character formation. Character traits in object relations theories have not consisted simply of drive and ego derivatives or the product of cultural processes, as the interpersonal psychoanalytic theorists claimed. Object relations views of character can be synthesized as having three simultaneous components. Character consists of: first, the person's patterns of attachment and relatedness, second, the template of one's inner world, and third, the repetition of the individual's object relational patterns. For Klein (1935, 1946) character began strictly as the template of the inner world, but it evolved into the ego's ties to the object world, according to Winnicott (1953, 1954) Fairbairn (1954) and Guntrip (1968). The development of object relational patterns takes place intrapsychicly in terms of symbolic fantasies which reflect the earliest primitive anxieties. Character traits and defenses have been seen as layers of protection against the earliest terrors of annihilation and psychotic anxiety. Neurotic character traits have been found to contain largely defensive responses to psychotic anxieties. The primary defense of dissociation underlies all character consolidation, and dissociation, at least for Winnicott, gave rise to false self organization. The interpersonal psychoanalytic and object relations models of character both embraced the importance of relational patterns and interpersonal transactions, although Sullivan did not express any sympathy for the concept of the internalized object.

Interpersonal Theories of Character

Character and the ego were both included under the term, the self system, in Sullivan's (1953) interpersonal psychoanalytic theory. The self system consisted of the individual's patterned system of knowledge and organization of experience (Thompson, 1978). Unlike classical Freudian theory's reliance on ego deficits and drives as the essence of character, in interpersonal theory, the manifestations of character always stemmed from the effects of interpersonal relations and culture. Horney (1937, 1939) developed the first comprehensive neoFreudian, cultural psychoanalytic theory of character. In her writings in the 1930's and 1940's Horney (1945, 1950) presented a systematic view of culture as both the force which underlies repression and the origin of neurotic traits and symptoms. Sullivan and Fromm felt that culture and chance happenings had a profound effect on character. Fromm (1941, 1947) surpassed Sullivan's view of culture by arguing that each society gives birth to and rewards those character traits which are necessary for its survival. A dialectic tension was described by Fromm (1973) between aloneness and the need for belonging which generated distinct character trends, such as those of the marketing personality and the necrophilic personality. The emphasis in Sullivan's theory was placed on those idiosyncratic capacities and developmental tendencies which gave shape to character.

In contrast to classical Freudian theory in which the level of libidinal fixation determined character, in Sullivan's interpersonal schema, each developmental stage had influential and potentially curative effects on character. All of the developmental stages, particularly the adolescent stages, were capable of having extremely positive effects on character, and of correcting previous deficits in the person's needs and functioning. Preadolescence offered psychotherapeutic possibilities in this developmental outline, because its facilitation of the chumship was accompanied by the longing for interpersonal intimacy. Character traits were composed of organized responses to the world and to anxiety, which were always interpersonal in origin. Defenses and symptoms of psychopathology did not represent drive based compromise formations. They were the products of interpersonal and familial processes.

Based on the ideas of Sullivan, Fromm and Horney, an overall summary of the interpersonal psychoanalytic views of character can be made as follows. Character refers to the psychic organization of experience which gives personality a unique pattern. This pattern evolves through the course of family transactions, interpersonal relationships, and the negotiation of developmental stages. The organization of character patterns involves misperceptions of interpersonal events, in what Sullivan first labelled, "a mystification of experience". The individual's pattern of misperceptions corresponds to defensive styles which become fixed during adolescence. Similarly, Shapiro (1965, 1981) hypothesized from a Freudian perspective that neurotic styles extend one's mode of perception and thought. As an outgrowth of interpersonal theory, the characterological approaches to integrating thought and affect were classified, by Barnett (1978, 1980A), as being either implosive or explosive. Implosive character types,

Barnett theorized, included the obsessional, the paranoid and the depressive who discharge affect inwardly in ways that disorganize logical syntactic thought. Explosive character types, which included the hysteric, the impulsive and the acting out character, discharge affect outwardly in ways that disorganize awareness of moods and meaningful verbal expression. In interpersonal theory the patterns of character are thus impassioned by the person's unique cognitive, affective method of knowing oneself and interacting with others.

Psychoanalytic Inquiry and The Effects of Trauma

Samuel Johnson noted that the biographer's task often involves touching lightly on those performances in life which reveal vulgar greatness. The psychoanalyst's task consists of creating the conditions for the simultaneous writing of the patient's emotional biography and the relinquishment of the patient's unhealthy character traits. Explorations of adolescent experience during adult analysis provide clarity about the impact of traumatic memories and childhood incidents which imprint characterological tendencies. The original Freudians believed that character was fully determined as an outcome of the Oedipus Complex. According to the classical Freudian model, developmental changes and life experience during adolescence were of secondary importance. Primary significance was attributed to the instinctual drives and the unconscious repetitions of Oedipal dramas. In fact, Freud and Ernest Jones both stated directly that the second decade of life amounted to a recapitulation of Oedipal development during the first five years. Nevertheless, Freud (1920, 1926) increased the scope of his concept of traumatic anxiety to include the ego's sense of helplessness in the face of both intrapsychic danger and environmental trauma. In Freud's (1926) view, the pervasive anxiety of traumatic experiences included all of the following dangers: the fear of annihilation, the fear of the loss of the object, castration anxiety, the fear of the loss of object love, and the fear of the loss of the superego's love. Khan (1974) observed that one traumatic event seldom gives definitive shape to the child's character formation. Based on Freud's seminal ideas about traumatic situations, Khan formed an appreciation of the disruptive effect on the child of the normal failures of the mother's role as a protective shield. According to Khan, the adult remembered repetitive family interactions as the essence of childhood trauma. His concept of "cumulative trauma" did not downplay the significance of genuine childhood tragedies, as much as it suggested that the ways in which we symbolize trauma make a statement about our character pathology.

The organization of symbolic memories is given its final shape, during adolescence, when introspection and abstraction ability are greatly enhanced. During adolescence, character traits provide the mechanisms for coping with both ongoing trauma and traumatic memories. I am suggesting that, during adolescence, character can be fully discerned as the filter through which trauma is symbolized. Each psychoanalytic model investigates the characterological impact of trauma in ways which define its clinical practice. The classical Freudian analyst attends to characterological expressions of resistance both inside and outside of the transference while becoming more aware of the patient's drive conflicts. To use Winnicott's phrase, the analyst facilitates the patient's wait for the "awakening of the true self" while he or she makes use of the analyst-mother to satisfy developmental needs. The interpersonal psychoanalyst constructs an inquiry about the diadic conscious and unconscious processes of exchange in order to articulate dissociated experience. However, traumatic memories are slanted in characterological directions which are unique to the individual, whatever the psychoanalytic model of investigation.

The psychoanalytic theories of development have made it clear that, during adolescence, character assumes psychic functions which had earlier been defensive aspects of the ego or the self. Before proceeding with a discussion of the psychoanalytic theories of adolescence, and before touching on an example of the use of memories of trauma to decipher character formation, I would first like to briefly contrast simplified Freudian, interpersonal and object relations conceptions of the goals of psychoanalysis. For Freud and Freudian theorists, the transference neurosis was the seemless core of the psychoanalytic situation, and the perspective from which object relationships and character trends were assessed. As symptom neuroses gradually began to be understood in theory and practice as extensions of character neuroses, character traits and symptoms were examined in the light of transference. After modifying his original declaration that the goal of psychoanalysis was to replace id processes with the ego, Freud (1933) reconstructed his theory of transference repetition. He concluded that the goal of clinical psychoanalysis was always to replace the patient's neurosis with the transference neurosis. The original infantile neurosis was given its voice in the transference neurosis with the analyst. Within the classical Freudian model, the ultimate psychoanalytic goal remained the resolution of the transference neurosis, and with it, the resolution of the Oedipus Complex. The classical analyst's strategy alternated between using the patient's free associations to uncover id derived conflicts and providing insight.   With the advent of ego psychology, character assessment emphasized resistance and defenses. However, it was the analysis and resolution of transference neurosis that allowed for substantial character change (Freud, 1940).

As was the case with interpersonal psychoanalytic theorists, character change for the object relations theorists, demanded tolerating the anxiety which is necessary for defining oneself in relation to others on the most basic level. According to the relational model, the patient must both experience and relinquish his or her contribution to the maintenance of the disordered internal world. For several British object relations theorists, especially Winnicott and Fairbairn, the goal of psychoanalysis was specifically to aid patients in giving up their closed system of inner reality. The new reality which was sought was one in which the patient was able to relate fully while using others appropriately. The psychoanalytic cure, for Winnicott (1965, 1989), involved the analyst taking on the maternal role in a replacement for the deficiencies of mother-infant bonding. The analyst served as a receptacle for the patient's psychopathology and deprivation induced hatred while correcting the deficits in early mothering. Character change came about as the result of support and maternal care in the transference. Character change in Winnicott's conceptual framework amounted to the enhanced capacity to play and, what he called, the true self's return from dissociation. This return could not be accomplished without the abandonment of pathological object relations patterns and the attainment of freedom from primitive anxiety. As a result, for Winnicott, the analyst's strategy alternated between affirmation of the patient's authenticity and gratification of the patient's developmental needs.

For contemporary Freudians and followers of Sullivan's interpersonal methods, tolerating anxiety and profiting from anxiety-provoking experience have become important goals for the psychoanalytic exploration of character. Blos (1979), for example, presented a cogent picture of the healthy adolescent as a youngster who can tolerate a measure of anxiety and depression without severe regression. The two-fold goal of Sullivan's interpersonal model consisted of assisting the patient with the expansion of the self and also with the ability to benefit from present interpersonal experience. The interpersonal psychoanalyst does not so much interpret the transference neurosisas use the ever expanding dynamic processes in the analysis to help remove the obstacles to the patient's growth. Sullivan emphasized that healthy character change is accomplished when there is a decrease in the patient's distortions and an increase in emotional freedom and responsiveness. The mature adult, according to Sullivan, has much in common with the fortunate adolescent, because both are able to make use of consensual validation in furthering self-awareness and profiting from healthy life experience. Each conquers the pain of loneliness while giving up egocentricity in favor of relatedness. The interpersonal psychoanalyst's main strategy consists of the utilization of directed free associations and the establishment of a detailed inquiry as a method of exploration. This inquiry expands incrementally to include not only what the patient has dissociated, but also the nuances of mutual influence in the patient-analyst interactions. For the Freudian, interpersonal psychoanalytic and object relations clinical models, the use of patient-analyst exchanges in transference-countertransference facilitates growth and change, even though such exchanges have different connotations in the different models. Yet, for all three models, as the patient's most profound anxieties are recreated with the analyst, character becomes less rigid, less dominated by internal objects and less governed by unhealthy defensive maneuvers.

Character Traits and Early Memories of Trauma

The Freudian, interpersonal and object relations theories of character have been in partial agreement that memories of trauma tend to disrupt healthy ego growth and the accomplishment of age appropriate development tasks. We know from Marcel Proust that memories obscure the certainty of death. The enveloping, protective shroud of memory distorts both past and present reality. Memories which symbolize childhood trauma are complexly organized in ways that shape character trends. Affect laden memories associated with early trauma have an enormous impact on the adult's relatedness and internalized relationships. Since affects such as guilt, shame, rage, helplessness and terror are frequently dissociated during traumatic experiences, they constrict relatedness and narrow the field of defensive operations. While single traumatic childhood events are often remembered accurately, ongoing trauma is more likely to induce characterological change (Terr, 1988). Early memories of trauma are embedded in the child's evolving use of symbols, and the retrieval of such memories is modified by defensive processes. Repressed memories of trauma organize character trends, as they are condensed with both earlier and later anxiety filled experiences. The following example illustrates the importance of primitive anxiety in character traits, as well as the defensive encoding of internalized relationships in a traumatic memory.

By the time he had the dream which will be mentioned below, the psychoanalyst Harry Guntrip had been in analysis with Fairbairn for about six years. Guntrip's autobiographical notes described the death of his younger brother, Percy, when Guntrip was three and one half years old, as the most decisive event of his life. According to Guntrip's family history, he found his dead brother on his mother's lap and then collapsed in a state of shock and silent withdrawal which threatened to become potentially fatal. Guntrip was fifty five years old and had long been suffering from an anxiety laden sense of unreality, when he had the following dream which he told to Fairbairn.

> I was going home from Edinburgh by train and had a lifesize dummy of a man left with me, made of flesh, human but no bones in it. I put it in the Guard's van to get rid of it, and propped it up as it slumped limp. I hurried away so the Guard wouldn't know it was mine. Not that was doing anything wrong but I didn't want him to know I had any connection with it. I met the Guard in the corridor and suddenly heard it shambling up after me, calling out. I felt a queer horror as if it was a sort of fleshly ghost, and said to the guard, "Quick, let's get away. It's alive. It'll get us." (Hughes, 1989).

Guntrip's association to the dream was that it represented his passive self presented to Fairbairn. Fairbairn apparently interpreted that this was the self which Guntrip's mother had suppressed. Guntrip described his mother as being highly abusive and rejecting. The treatment was seemingly only partially successful in freeing Guntrip from the effects of his mother's unresponsiveness by its analysis in the transference with Fairbairn (Guntrip, 1975).

In the course of Fairbairn's (1952) writing on dreams, he stressed that each element in a dream represents the dreamer and the dreamer's object seeking. Guntrip admitted that his amplification of Fairbairn's theory of primitive anxiety in schizoid states had much of its source in his own feelings of unreality and detachment. Classical psychoanalysts might hear a number of themes in the dream, such as an Oedipal crime, the fear of ego disintegration, or the fear of sadism, as partial explanations for Guntrip's anxiety and obsessional traits. By his own acknowledgment, Guntrip's schizoid anxiety contained elements of paralyzing fear, intense depression and acute loneliness. According to his own account, Guntrip spent many hundreds of hours making detailed notes on both of his analyses. Hazell's (1991) report of his analysis with Guntrip documented Guntrip's obsessional thinking and complete intolerance of patients' silence, prior to the period of his second analysis with Winnicott. In the dream, Guntrip feared being pursued by the dummy of a man, which might have represented his own longlasting isolation and detachment. Guntrip was also afraid of the guard or the authority's disapproval, and the guard was equated with the analyst. In addition, if the zombie-like lifeless shell of the dummy symbolized the analyst as object, then the analyst was devalued as weak, and limp, or in other words, castrated and impotent. Since train journeys signify themes of anxiety about separation and differentiation, Guntrip might have been signaling that his passivity and his states of isolation and inertia were dynamically related to either a fear of merger with the malevolent analyst mother, or a fear of leaving the denigrated analyst father.

Interpersonal and object relations approaches to the analysis of the dream would cultivate the theme of terror and horror implicit in the symbolized internalized relationships and the therapeutic interaction. Guntrip felt that the dream captured the trauma of his brother's death. More powerful still was the dream's imaginative reshaping of his defensive flight from the fear of vitality, along with his possible use of dissociation and splitting in the reenactment of his relational patterns. The depictions of people in relationships in the dream were anchored in images of a terrified victim and a lifeless, spineless dummy. If Guntrip or Fairbairn had associations to the dummy of either a ventriloquist's dummy, or the British use of the word, dummy, for a pacifier, then the dream took on additional significance. In light of the former association, the latent content would soar with a sadomasochistic relatedness in which Guntrip unconsciously permitted and sought being dominated and controlled. The latter association would suggest the possibility of the internalization of the earliest maternal neglect and abuse. In the case of either association, the propping up of the dummy-ghost might have signified Guntrip's donning the costume of schizoid withdrawal in order to avoid the dread of individuation from his internal objects. The terrifying image of the fleshy ghost coming to life provided illustrative support for the hypothesis that primitive annihilation anxiety stems from ambivalence about separation and mourning of internal objects. The efficacy of this hypothesis, and the power of the adolescent maturational process to evoke primitive anxiety, will be reviewed in subsequent theoretical and clinical chapters.

Psychoanalysts who focus on countertransference might wonder how Guntrip's dream correlated with his presence, and how it broadcast that he was making a *dummy* out of his analyst. Was Guntrip in fact making a fool out of Fairbairn by insisting that his passive self be acknowledged? Was this passive self really one which had been completely destroyed in childhood? Was he reenacting his own victimization and identification with the aggressor by being sadistic and robbing himself of his own vitality? Had Fairbairn unconsciously colluded with Guntrip's self-devaluation and efforts to get away from the analysis? Answers to these questions might have been provided either by Fairbairn's asking for further associations or by his making a directive statement such as: Tell me about the horror!

In their writings both Fairbairn and Guntrip were highly adept at commenting on the subjective experience of primitive anxiety. Hazell (1991) reported that Guntrip continued to be troubled by disabling feelings of exhaustion well into his sixties until his reanalysis with Winnicott. In the course of conversations with Landis (1981), Guntrip volunteered that the deadly atmosphere in his family was the most serious problem in his developmental history. Hughes's (1989) discussion of Guntrip's life contributed the information that he was viciously beaten as a young child, and that he was forced to wear girls' dresses until his mother's shop customers raised objections. Guntrip's (1975) own report of his two analyses credited Winnicott's empathic responsiveness with rescuing his infant self and bringing it to life from an apathetic withdrawal which had begun long before Percy's death. Fairbairn's clinical notes on his patients suggested his awareness of some of the dynamic questions I have raised. Sutherland (1989), Fairbairn's biographer, indicated that Fairbairn's analysis of Guntrip helped to crystallize not only his concept of the anti-libidinal ego, but also his ideas about characterological retreat from internal objects.

Conclusion

My assessment of Guntrip's dream has touched on the characterological linkage between primitive anxiety and ambivalence about mourning internal objects - a point which has been made in different theoretical terms by Blos, Fairbairn, Fromm, Klein and Searles. My interpretative comments about the dream have drawn upon the pluralism of the classical Freudian, interpersonal and object relations concepts of character formation. Memories which are given their organization by trauma skew character consolidation in particular directions. Traumatic memories are recreated in analysis by the reenactment of unconscious relational patterns and dissociated affects. Guntrip's dream served to reinforce the contention that character traits cannot be simply designated as fixed entities of psychic structure and defense. Each of the psychoanalytic models of metapsychology has exceeded Reich's libidinal formulation that character consisted of the ego's defensive armour against the repressed. Whether predominantly obsessional, paranoid, hysterical, depressive, narcissistic, schizoid, antisocial or borderline, character trends are now understood as the products of internalized relationships and encapsulated experience. An integration of the three psychoanalytic theoretical models suggests that character traits express processes which combine depictions of who a person is with what he or she does with others. The maturational changes of adolescence usher in the conditions for character consolidation.

In subsequent chapters, my main objectives will be to further contrast the three principal psychoanalytic models of character consolidation and to use concepts from each model in order to assess the role of primitive anxiety states in adolescent character disturbance. Part I of this work will contain a historical review of the psychoanalytic theories of adolescent character formation, as well as a discussion of the role of both primitive anxiety and abusive families in character consolidation. Part II will include chapters which will explore primitive anxiety or annihilation anxiety in psychoanalytic theory and analytic treatment. In Part III, specific forms of adolescents' character and identity pathology will be examined. Since my focus will deliberately be on adolescents with psychotic, borderline, violent, and narcissistic character features, my approach will neither follow a precise outline of psychoanalytic developmental theories, nor offer a complete overview of character typology. The preponderance of primitive anxiety states and regressed forms of relatedness will be stressed in severe types of character disturbance. The final chapter of this volume will consist of a detailed case study of adolescent narcissism in which a combination of ego attitudes and family processes gave rise to the need to become the object of tantalizing fascination.

CHAPTER TWO

Adolescent Development
and
Psychoanalytic Theory

Adolescence is a developmental disturbance.

Anna Freud

A significant encounter can modify earlier traumas.

Harry Stack Sullivan

The psychoanalytic theories of adolescence emanated from a philosophy of development which had been radicalized by Freud's heralding of infantile sexuality. In contrast to his American contemporary, G. Stanley Hall, Freud wrote relatively little about the personality transformations of adolescence. Although the *Standard Edition* of Freud's complete works contained surprisingly few references to adolescence, Freud definitively made known the importance of puberty in the resurgence of the Oedipus Complex and the instinctual drives. As I stated in the previous chapter, the three psychoanalytic models cast developmental processes in the light of their divergent theories. In this chapter, an assessment will be made of the similarities and differences between the Freudian, interpersonal, and object relations theorists' views of adolescent development. I will also begin to elaborate the theme that adolescents' anxieties and depressive states manifest their dread of the annihilation of the self and the object. My focus on character etiology will not include an overview of character typology, and it will limit my discussion of sexuality and identity, even though these are the principal themes of adolescents' psychological reorganization. Moreover, I will also refer to aspects of the first analysis of an adolescent, Freud's case of Dora, in order to compare the clinical implications of the three chief psychoanalytic theoretical models. Despite their far reaching differences in metapsychology, the clinical theories of each analytic orientation have evolved to a point of some convergence in the treatment of adolescents.

Introduction

Guntrip (1961), in his critical analysis of structural theory, pointed out the limitations of comparisons of psychoanalytic developmental models. Theoretical comparisons, such as the one I am about to undertake, are hampered by the lack of uniformity of metapsychological terms in the different psychoanalytic theories. Concepts like the ego, identity, and the object have varied greatly across theories in their scientific and descriptive levels of meaning. The enormous range of the psychoanalytic theories of adolescent character formation precludes intense scrutiny, in this chapter, of adolescents' gender differences, their sexual development, their specific age-related developmental tasks and other crucial topics. Nevertheless, in spite of these limitations, as a way of contrasting the Freudian, interpersonal and object relations developmental models, I will first introduce and then survey key aspects of the psychologies of adolescence of Freud, Anna Freud, Erikson, Blos, Sullivan, Fromm, Winnicott and other theorists. In the later part of this chapter, my discussion of material from the analysis of Dora will stress that the contemporary Freudian, interpersonal and object relations clinical theories are congruent to the extent that they underscore the analytic task of facilitating individuation from internal objects.

According to Freud (1905A), the aftereffects of puberty had the greatest bearing on the restructuring of psychological development and the final delineation of character. Freud depicted psychosexual development as a genetically determined process. It was influenced, only secondarily, by the family or the culture, and by the nature of the adolescent's internalized object relations. For Freud, adolescents' final sexual organization corresponded to the consolidation of character. Sullivan's interpersonal approach to adolescence placed a much greater emphasis on culture and cognitive maturation than was present in Freud's theory of adolescent development. According to Sullivan's developmental model, the adolescent stages represented an epoch of great hopefulness and potential personality change. For Sullivan, the adolescent attained character consolidation with the increased complexity of his or her organization of experience. Emotional maturity, during adolescence, was signalled by the degree of healthy involvement in interpersonal experience. For the British object relations theorists, adolescents' character changes emerged from the interplay of drive conflicts with the continuation of earlier object relations patterns. Although Melanie Klein's object relations approach departed from Freudian theory, her concentration on character trends, like that of Freud, emphasized the child's intrapsychic fantasy life. For Fairbairn, Winnicott, Guntrip and Khan, adolescence was seen as the stage when disturbed ego processes and schizoid (or primitive) anxiety resulted in more visible signs of ego pathology. Each of these four theorists wrote about adolescent patients' object relations in ways which took into account the role of both family experience and the internalized objects.

The centrality of an interpersonal, object relations basis for character formation has been discussed extensively by many authors who have noted the shift away from the purely intrapsychic in psychoanalytic personality theory. Barnett (1978,1980B), for example, continued the interpersonal tradition of Horney, Sullivan, Fromm and Clara Thompson with his observation that the self, and its expression in character, was manifest in all of the person's transactions with others. Mitchell (1988) summarized contemporary, interactional views of character by noting that, what he called, the psychoanalytic relational models included the interpersonal, the self psychology and the object relations perspectives.

The Freudian Theory of Adolescence

The classical psychoanalytic investigation of adolescence began with Freud's *Three Essays on Sexuality which was* published in 1905. In these essays, Freud affirmed the crucial significance of infantile sexuality for adolescents' establishment of new sexual objects and new sexual aims. Here, as in other writings, he stated that character was basically determined by the outcome of the Oedipal period. As a result of puberty, infantile sexuality fell into its final form in such a way that the adolescent's instinctual life became subordinated to the genitals. At puberty, Freud suggested, increased stimulation of the erotogenic zones coincided with the attainment of genital primacy and an intensification of libido, since the adolescent was capable of finding an appropriate sexual object. Following puberty, a readjustment of defenses was necessary because of the revival of Oedipal fantasies and attachments. Due to their increased instinctual conflicts, adolescents were said to make considerable use of repression, as well as, reaction formation and sublimation. The course of earlier Oedipal development determined the individual's psychological progress throughout adolescence. However, except in cases of what Freud considered to be disturbances of psychosexual development, adolescents' pleasure seeking entailed a detachment from the incestuous Oedipal objects. These changes in adolescents' sexual organization, together with the renewed resolution of the Oedipus Complex, conjured up the tasks of character consolidation.

Adolescent developmental changes in sexual identity and masturbation fantasies were also formulated by Freud. According to his theoretical approach, a reorientation of the body ego and a consolidation of the sexual identity took place during adolescence. As a result of the simultaneous revival and repudiation of Oedipal longings, a detachment from parental authority was likewise said to occur. Although changes in adolescents' object relations were contained in Freud's outline of adolescence, adolescents' object relations patterns were more fully discussed by Anna Freud, Peter Blos and Edith Jacobson. Beginning with Freud's statements, masturbation fantasies were investigated as essential reflections of adolescent development. Freud theorized that, as the agent of infantile sexuality, masturbation took on additional significance following adolescents' intensification of their instinctual drives. Masturbation reorganized adolescents' sexual fantasies in accordance with their erotic attachments and the prospect of genitality. As an outgrowth of Freud's theory, later Freudian theorists, especially Erikson, refocused psychosexual development to reflect adolescents' ego changes and establishment of a more stable identity.

Adolescents' difficulties with giving up Oedipal ties were considered, in classical Freudian theory, as crucial to the origins of psychopathology. More contemporary Freudian theorists have expanded the exploration of middle and late adolescence, together with these stages' activation of mood shifts and pre-Oedipal conflicts (Esman 1980; Jacobson, 1961). Their descriptions of adolescents' failures to relinquish Oedipal bonds have exceeded Freud's focus on puberty, as the definitive experience which provided sexuality with its final shape. Ernest Jones (1922) summarized Freud's original view of adolescence with the succinct statement that it represented the recapitulation of Oedipal development.

This idea-that infantile sexuality fixed the course of adolescent psychic development - was reiterated in the early psychoanalytic papers on adolescent treatment and character disturbance. Freudian approaches to analytic treatment with adolescents evolved from Freud's view of adolescence as primarily a transitional stage to adult sexuality. Freud's writings only partially emphasized adolescents' emotional lability and their process of disengagement in pursuit of a personal identity.

Anna Freud conducted the first analytic work with children, and she provided the first complete psychoanalytic report of adolescents' emotional instability. Anna Freud's major contributions to the subject of adolescence began with her observations about the curtailment of the truce between the ego and id at the end of the latency period. Her accounts of adolescents' personality reorganization placed great emphasis on regression which stemmed from the need to repudiate Oedipal wishes. She believed that adolescent patients provided analysis with the clearest picture of the dynamic role of both anxiety and the failure of repression in mental breakdown. Her impression that adolescents had only a limited ability to form transferences due to their minimal libidinal investment in the analyst, led to questions about the suitability of adolescents for the psychoanalytic procedure. In her (1937) seminal work on the ego, she advocated the analysis of defenses before content, and she championed the view that the ego deals with reality conflicts, not just drives. The degree of importance Anna Freud placed on adolescents' regression had the cumulative effect of dominating the classical Freudian conception of adolescent development.

In her 1958 paper, *Adolescence,* Anna Freud discussed adolescents' defensive processes as the basis for the consolidation of character traits. By highlighting the defenses, which adolescent patients used in their libidinal conflicts, she continued Freud's concept of symptoms as compromise accommodations with the drives. In particular, she identified three defensive processes as central to the adolescent's character formation. These defensive operations included the displacement of libido, for example in romanticized crushes, reversal of affect or reaction formation, and regression or withdrawal of libido into the self. As a result of the equation Anna Freud made between adolescence and developmental disturbance, the Freudian theory of adolescence illuminated the closeness of adolescents' emotional volatility to the signs of illness. Adolescents' emotional lability, their susceptibility to anxiety, and their contradictory emotional states were thus all understood as approximations to symptoms. Anna Freud's description of the incapacities of narcissistic and borderline patients, as problems in early development, was highly influential in increasing the scope of psychoanalytic patient populations. Her suggestions about the analysis of adolescents' resistances were based on great sensitivity to adolescents' fears of their regressive tendencies. She believed that if the analyst was able to formulate a treatment alliance, then adolescent patients could be assisted with restoration to the path of normal development. Anna Freud's theoretical writings on adolescence elaborated Freud's view that instincts from childhood developmental phases persisted in the libidinal foundation of character. In her theory, the relative success or failure of defenses against Oedipal and pre-Oedipal object ties largely determined the outcome of character. The image she presented, of the highly rebellious, regressed adolescent, in great mental distress, has been challenged by a number of theorists, such as Masterson (1967, 1974), who have questioned its universality. In general, classical Freudian theorists' accounts of adolescence have stressed the final structuring of the personality in relation to Oedipal wishes, and the increased complexity of the ego which takes place with the recognition of the tasks of adulthood (Ritvo, 1971).

Ego Psychology and Adolescence

Erik Erikson and Peter Blos both extended Freud's instinctual theory of adolescence, as well as Anna Freud's focus on ego processes during adolescent development. Erikson's work was enlivened by his association with Anna Freud in Vienna. In his theoretical papers and imaginative biographies, Erikson orchestrated a comprehensive psychological approach to adolescent development. By emphasizing the ego's concerns with reality and society, he embellished drive theory, while he created a link to the suppositions of interpersonal theory and object relations theories. Erikson combined psychosexual theory with Anna Freud's ideas about defenses in his well known sequence of the epigenetic stages of human life. In the late 1970's Erikson admitted that the developmental tasks of these detailed epigenetic stages could not be fully realized in any one life stage, since the bases for their accomplishment lay in all of the stages. For Erikson, the psychosexual stages concerned zones for relating to objects, and they entailed unconscious expressions of the child's needs.   His psychoanalytic psychology of adolescence was based on the twofold importance of identity formation and the ego's adjustments to the drives and to society.

Erikson's writings on adolescence addressed both the anxiety inherent in the process of identity formation, and the analytic task of helping the adolescent to assess values and choices from the point of view of identity synthesis.   In contrast to Anna Freud's concern with adolescents' regression, Erikson emphasized adolescents' unfolding maturation and adaptation.   In contrast to the interpersonal theorists' belief that cultural forces produced the manifestations of psychopathology, Erikson stressed the influence of societal factors on the ego.   Although he retained the tenets of drive theory, Erikson shared the interpersonal theorists' interest in the effect of social forces on psychological adjustment.   In terms which reiterated a point that had been made previously by W. Reich, Erikson stated that a society's values had a great impact on the individual's character traits.   Neuroses, he felt, or other types of disorders, were expressed in the mental concerns, as well as the physical, and social, attitudes of the person.   However, it was the drives which accounted for the enhancement of the child's object relations, and the development of his or her ego capacities.   The touchstones of Erikson's developmental theory attributed the dynamics of human behavior to the effects of maturational processes, which, he summarized, as man's biopsychosocial unity.

Throughout decades of his work, Erikson crafted a portrait of the emotional, sexual and social aspects of the process of coming of age.   In an early (1956) paper on ego synthesis and a later work on the subject of youth, Erikson (1968A) presented a picture of identity growth as stemming from transitory identity crises.   During adolescence, these passing disturbances were capable of reaching temporary neurotic or psychotic proportions.   Identity crises occurred because infantile conflicts had to be reconciled with the complexities of later identifications. Through the concepts of the identity crisis and identity confusion or identity diffusion, Erikson, (like Sullivan) attempted to understand the poorly differentiated self and the unsuccessful adaptations of late adolescence.   Identity confusion was characterized by difficulties with "intimacy, industry and time perspective".   A number of authors, such as Kernberg (1976), have critized Erikson for not distinguishing the emotional distress of adolescence from the symptoms of serious identity diffusion which earmark the borderline personality disorder.   Because of

Erikson's reluctance to have young people labelled, as deviant, he argued that adolescents' acute depression, violence, and delinquency all might represent fleeting crises rather than signs of breakdown or character disturbance. Based on Erikson's criteria, follow up studies of adolescents, who exhibited severe identity confusion, have reported its far from transitory nature (Josselson, 1987).

In a highly important paper on identity, Erikson (1968B) contrasted the subjective sense of personal continuity with those aspects of identity which have both individual and social components. His concept of the ego identity referred to both continuity over time and to inner continuity in the face of social patterns and the drives. What Erikson called, psychosocial identity, was determined by the end of the adolescent period. This latter process of identity formation included the repudiation and assimilation of childhood identifications in a configuration which relied on societal recognition. As a more or less completed process, identity formation thus included the adolescent's most vibrant values and world views which were backed up by societal ideals. Early adulthood signified both a mental maturity and a sexual maturity which coincided with the seeking of new partners and goals. Erikson's (1959A, 1959B) papers on late adolescence affirmed the active searching for ideals and self images which characterize this developmental stage. The body of Erikson's work pointedly captured adolescents' growing awareness of their personal history and their emergent sense of "I". His theoretical emphasis on adolescents' identity formation has been continued by other Freudian theorists who have connected identity formation with the continuity of self representations (Sandler, 1981). However, by making ego enhancement and the establishment of the identity the essential tasks of adolescence, Erikson set his theory apart from those theoretical models which emphasized interpersonal or object relations patterns during adolescence. What Erikson included under the study of identity, other psychoanalytic theorists discussed as issues of character disturbance and the psychopathology of object relations.

Blos (1962, 1977, 1979) applied Mahler's theory of separation-individuation, and its concentration on ego development, to the adolescent period. His descriptions of adolescents' object relations and his clinical insights have provided major contributions to Freudian developmental theory. Blos assessed adolescent's changes in object relations in terms of both separation anxiety and the mourning of the preOedipal parents as lost love objects. His (1967, 1968) notion of identity formation was that the more or less completed identity resulted from the integration of self representations into the remainder of the ego. Based on his extensive clinical experience, Blos articulated the goals of analytic treatment for adolescent patients in developmental terms. Successful analytic therapy required the patient's ability to tolerate a degree of anxiety and depression, in addition to the recognition of conflicts and self-deceptions. The most complex, difficult therapeutic goal consisted of assisting the adolescent patient with the deidealization of the self and the deidealization of the object. The mourning of the parents and the reworking of Oedipal conflicts inevitably entered into the treatment process. Blos suggested that adolescents' striving for independence from the internalized objects, constituted the second separation-individuation process. Like Anna Freud, Blos maintained that adolescents inevitably regress in order to face their infantile conflicts with internal objects. In accordance with Freud's models of mental life, Blos hypothesized that adolescence draws a line of demarcation between character traits and character synthesis. Like Anna Freud, he saw adolescents' impulsivity and their idealism as evanescent characteristics. According to Blos's clinical approach, analytic treatment with adolescents demanded a lengthy course of therapy. Their difficulty in forming the transference neurosis created impediments to a full analysis of their transference states. Blos (1980) summarized his view of adolescent maturation as consisting of the attainment of ego continuity together with the disengagement from Oedipal and preOedipal ties. The basic aim of analytic therapy, for adolescents, consisted of the redirection of the developmental process.

Blos discussed character synthesis during adolescence from two vantagepoints. In his clinical studies, he consistently listened for evidence suggestive of symptoms in formation as a prelude to character disturbance. In several theoretical papers, he outlined aspects of character formation which were mostly completed by the end of adolescence. Based on the model of Freud, Abraham and Reich, Blos (1968) traced the evolution of adolescents' drive fixations into character trends. Character synthesis referred to the structural changes which ended adolescence. The preconditions for this final stage of character formation included the establishment of ego continuity, and the sexual identity, as well as the loosening of preOedipal object ties. Blos conceived of character synthesis as involving the broadening of the ego's autonomy and its ability to handle the aftereffects of trauma. Residual trauma was the chief organizing force in adolescent character formation.

Character was therefore synonymous with the pattern of the adolescent's responses and evolving adaptations to signal anxiety. A brief summary of this aspect of Blos's voluminous work, which has current implications, was contained in his statement that character consisted of the person's ongoing adaptation to residual trauma.

The conceptual landscape of Freud's psychoanalytic theory of adolescence has also been greatly enriched by M. and E. Laufer's (1968, 1981, 1984) reports of developmental breakdown in adolescent disturbance. The Laufers combined Freud's concentration on puberty, and Anna Freud's concept of developmental lines, with their own idea that a breakdown in the developmental process, specifically in the sexual identity, was the crucial dimension of adolescent psychopathology. They have consistently noted that the adolescent's distorted relationship with his or her sexual body becomes manifest in pregenital masturbation fantasies. This disturbed relationship with the sexual body represents the primary obstacle to the developmental process.   Under these circumstances, a poor integration into mature genitality takes place, with expressions of shame, and rejection, or even hatred, of the sexual body.

For the Laufers, the developmental breakdown constitutes the central aspect of adolescents' psychopathology.   This kind of breakdown potentially includes attacks on both the internalized parent and the sexual body.   Such expressions of self-hatred have been noted in adolescents' addictions, their eating disorders, and their suicidal self-destructiveness. The Laufers (1976,1978) advocated treatment principles based on their exploration of the rigidity of adolescents' defenses, and whether or not the defenses allow for any developmental progress.   In their view, the analytic experience facilitates adolescents' detachment from their parents in addition to their resolution of earlier Oedipal conflicts.

The Laufers, Blos, Erikson and Anna Freud all expanded Freud's vision of infantile sexuality as the cornerstone of adolescents' character formation and the ultimate source of the ego's increased influence over the id and the superego.

Interpersonal Theories of Adolescence

Sullivan's (1940, 1954, 1956) concepts of anxiety and sexuality placed him at great odds with the Freudian view of adolescent development. His analysis of the pain of his own adolescent years influenced both his theoretical model and his clinical theory of psychotherapy. The loneliness and prejudice Sullivan endured led to his identification of culture, and the family, as the determinants of psychopathology. I have already mentioned that, as an outgrowth of Sullivan's sensitivity to primitive anxiety, he hypothesized that adolescence was the stage of the greatest closeness to schizophrenia. Sullivan achieved highly effective therapeutic results with adolescent schizophrenic patients. His one-genus postulate enhanced his assumption that the knowledge of psychotic processes was universal, especially during adolescence. His belief that adolescent warps in interpersonal relationships created unhealthy character trends illustrated the neoFreudian belief in the cultural sources of neurotic conflicts. The cultural approach to neurotic character formation was shared by Horney and Fromm. Sullivan's view of anxiety, as always being interpersonal in its origin and manifestations, bore a close resemblance to both Horney's (1937, 1939, 1951) concept of basic anxiety and Fromm's concept of existential anxiety as the underlying sources of neurotic character. Fromm (1941, 1947) cautioned that attributing libidinal terms to character traits missed the essential role of the child or adolescent's life experience and family environment. Fromm held that character provided the young person with a distinct identity and a frame of orientation for life. Character evolved through culturally based processes of socialization and assimilation. Unhealthy, destructive character trends, like violence or excessive acquisitiveness, corresponded to both impaired relatedness and the surrender of individuality. According to Fromm, all pathological character traits arose from man's fear of aloneness. The healthy adolescent or adult embraced existential anxiety as a choice over the neurotic, nonproductive types of character orientation (such as the hoarding, exploitative or receptive characters). Sexuality especially registered the extent of the individual's character problems and degree of self-alienation. Singer (1965) extended Fromm's theoretical position, with his belief that sexuality expressed the interpersonal aspects of an individual's pathology. According to Sullivan, primitive anxiety played its key role in character formation by creating disabling states of panic and incapacities in interpersonal relations. Like the other interpersonal theorists, Sullivan suggested that neither childhood, nor adolescent trauma indelibly shaped character, because life events had a reparative effect on all developmental stages. In keeping with his hopeful outlook, Sullivan concluded that the adolescent stages, particularly preadolescence, proffered the greatest opportunities for the corrections of the deficiencies of prior developmental stages. Within this interpersonal, humanistic model, adolescents' symptoms and character trends needed to the appreciated as adaptations to both neurotic values and the cultural environment.

In my view, the hopefulness implicit in Sullivan's theory of adolescence was expressed, not only in his developmental outline, but also in his clinical approach to psychotherapy. According to his interpersonal theory, the major developmental tasks of adolescence entailed the attainment of intimacy and the establishment of the lust dynamism. Sullivan (1953) defined lust, the felt aspects of sexuality, as including a pattern of overt and covert symbolic processes. These symbolic processes reflected deep-seated attitudes about oneself and others, rather than infantile sexuality. The negotiation of the tasks of lust and intimacy molded the adolescent's emotional and social adjustment. However, the characterological outcome of adolescence depended greatly upon chance factors, as well as socioeconomic variables, and cultural conditions. Perry (1982), for example, accented Sullivan's concerns, during the 1930's, about the effects of racial prejudice and antiSemitism on self-esteem and character development. Cultural pressures, which threatened security, were paramount in Sullivan's concept of anxiety. Sullivan's analytic method (which will be expanded later in this chapter and in the final chapter under the heading of participant observation) was embedded in his field theory-like perspective on development. His clinical approach with adolescents emphasized reducing their anxiety while evaluating the omissions and inconsistencies in their reported experience. The patient's developmental history provided the point of reference for his therapeutic inquiry. The prognostic outcome of therapy could be hopeful, for Sullivan, even with severe disturbances, because personality never remained fixed, either before or after adolescence. Sullivan alluded to this innate tendency as the tendency towards personality integration.

Object Relations Theories of Adolescence

The proflic writings of Klein, Fairbairn, Winnicott, Guntrip, and Khan, as well as those of other theorists, (Jacobson, Kernberg, Kohut, Mahler, Masterson, Rinsley, and Volkan) have conveyed object relations insights about development which are relevant to adolescent psychology. Because of the far-reaching scope of their portraits of illness and development, I will briefly review the contributions of only a few of these theorists. My approach to this topic will be limited to Winnicott's, Fairbairn's and Khan's ideas about adolescence, and it will not include a comprehensive summary of object relations theories.

Object relations theorists have provided elaborations of the effects of human relationships on all aspects of development and psychopathology. In an overview of object relations theories, Hamilton (1989) credited the use of object relations concepts with facilitating the analyses of individuals with many forms of severe disorders. Although Klein (1934, 1946) wrote relatively little about adolescence, she ascertained that disturbances of late adolescence continued the anxieties of the paranoid-schizoid and depressive positions. The groundwork for a distinct object relations theory of adolescence was contained in Winnicott's concepts of ego relatedness and the facilitating environment. Winnicott (1961, 1971) attributed adolescents' psychic disturbances to environmental failures, more than to specific forms of character pathology. Klein, Winnicott and Fairbairn all held that, throughout development, character trends expressed internalizations of (and defenses against) ties to bad object attachments. Unlike Klein, Fairbairn and later Guntrip rejected both the death instinct's primacy, and drive theory, in favor of object seeking as the fundamental source of human motivation. Guntrip (1969, 1971) classified the inner sense of individuality, which blossomed during adolescence, as one of the personality's basic needs. Khan contributed to an object relations theory of adolescence by his descriptions of sexuality, and by his discussion of adolescents' identity disturbance. In Khan's (1974, 1979) renewal of Winnicott's ideas, adolescents' lack of identity stemmed from disturbances in early body ego development and pathological identifications with the mother. Khan's view was that the latent emotionality of such early body ego experience found expression, during adulthood, in sexual intercourse and in the excitement of sexual perversions. Khan's discussions of his adolescent patients' affectivity elucidated Winnicott's use of countertransference with adolescents. According to each of these object relations theorists, I have mentioned, the repetitive feelings, inherent in internalized attachments, persisted in their influence on defenses during the predicaments of adolescence.

Winnicott (1956A, 1956B, 1958) linked ego relatedness, developmentally, with not only the baby's capacity to be alone, but also the baby's foundation of selfhood. The adolescent's relationship with the sexually maturing body reiterated this ego relatedness of mother-child body centered interactions. Winnicott's reports of his analytic work with adolescents kept in focus his objective of bolstering their development beyond the Oedipal level. This aim was achieved, with a number of Winnicott's adolescent patients, by his willingness to play and by his use of the squiggle game. Nevertheless, Winnicott's (1954A, 1954B, 1989) primary therapeutic goal with adolescents was always to make sure that the patient used the transference in order to overcome deprivations in maternal care.

Winnicott came to work with adolescent patients relatively late in his career as a psychoanalyst. His complex ideas on development seemed to include an apparent contradiction about the nature of adolescents' assertiveness or passivity in the emotional growth process. In agreement with Anna Freud, Winnicott (1962, 1965A, 1988) speculated that adolescents' disturbances were often indistinguishable from the problems they encountered on the way to independence. He assigned to the analyst the crucial task of maintaining complete subservience to the traumas which the patient needed to stage. For Winnicott, narcissistic and borderline traits expressed adolescent patients' underlying core experiences of unreality and madness. His pronouncements about these ego states of unreality resembled the interpersonal theorists' accounts of disturbed youths' bouts of disintegration. With schizoid adolescents, Winnicott especially allowed the patient the crucial opportunity to unconsciously create the psychoanalyst. In his discussion of adolescent immaturity, Winnicott (1986A) presented a hypothesis which outlined adolescents' essential involvement with the unconscious murder of their parents. This involvement was said to foster pubertal and postpubertal maturation. However, adolescents were depicted, elsewhere in Winnicott's writings, as fundamentally passive and reactive. Their psychic assertiveness was reduced to the passive status of remaining captive hostages of their peers and biological maturation. Winnicott (1965B) designated adolescents' negotiation of developmental tasks as a process of waiting "in the doldrums".

The ideas of Winnicott and Fairbairn were only partially compatible with Freud's psychosexual theory and his views of adolescence. Winnicott's underscoring of adolescents' unconscious destructiveness suggested that he endorsed a Kleinian view of adolescence. This emphasis on adolescents' murderous fantasies raised the possibility that his developmental theory fell into the same conceptual trap of diminishing the importance of the real family, for which he had criticized Klein.

However, Winnicott (1986B, 1987) acknowledged elsewhere-in an anti-Kleinian position - that analytic work with adolescents was ineffective without the presence of a healthy family which fostered maturation. These seemingly contradictory ideas about adolescent development did not culminate in a theory of adolescent character pathology which was as fully articulated as Winnicott's theories of infantile trauma. Fairbairn (1952, 1954) thoroughly developed the thesis that infantile splitting of the ego and the object accounted for adolescent and adult character traits. He attributed the underlying cause of all types of character disturbance to simultaneously exciting and rejecting parental attitudes. In Fairbairn's theory, drive conflicts represented zones or areas for the expression of personal relationships and internal object relations conflicts. The need to retreat from bad internalized images resulted in the adolescent's reliance on hysterical, obsessional, paranoid, depressive, and schizoid defenses. Each of the founders of object relations theories (Klein, Fairbairn, and Winnicott) thus placed considerable emphasis on the continuance of early defenses and anxiety laden relationships in adolescent character organization.

Summary

The foremost implication of the Freudian theories of adolescence has been that the analyst enters into an alliance with the patient's developmental process. During sessions, stock is routinely taken of the adolescent patient's defenses and drive fixations. The interpersonal and object relations theories of adolescents' character formation varied with each other and also with the assumptions of classical Freudian metapsychology. Yet, Sullivan, Fairbairn and Winnicott all stressed relatedness in character formation. They each urged that the attitudes of the actual person in significant relationships, as well as the internal representations of the self and the object, shaped the character tendencies of the child or adolescent. Sullivan was very outspoken about his belief that there could be no uniformly valid theory of character, because people are unique. However, for Sullivan, the needs for the validation of self worth, and for freedom from anxiety, were universal stimuli for the increasing organization of character trends. In both interpersonal theory and object relations theories, dissociative processes were of paramount importance, as defensive operations. Dissociation, by the adolescent, resulted in further instances of ego splitting (for Fairbairn), of the bad-me (for Sullivan), and of the false self (for Winnicott). Fairbairn, and to some extent Winnicott, used the language of classical Freudian theory in order to shape an object relations theory of adolescent development. In spite of their theoretical differences, Sullivan, Fairbairn and Winnicott spoke with a singular voice in dismissing the exclusive significance of libidinal fixations in character consolidation.

I now wish to review Freud's case of Dora as an addendum to this short critical appraisal. The analysis of Dora readily lends itself to a discussion of the confluence of the psychoanalytic models' clinical theories. Dora's unfortunate experience in treatment offered a compelling example of the precariousness of adolescents' adjustment in the midst of developmental and family turmoil.

Freud's Case of Dora

Freud's (1905B) study of Dora has been one of his most widely discussed and frequently criticized case monographs. As a result of this first analysis of an adolescent, Freud came to acknowledge and appreciate the importance of negative transference and resistance. So many theoretical papers have been written about Dora, that the limited scope of my objective will be to use the analysis of her first dream in order to contrast clinical implications of the Freudian, object relations and interpersonal theories of adolescence. This highly difficult case was not intended by Freud to be a treatise on psychoanalytic technique, and it introduced the complications imposed by his analytic work with adolescents. My specific aim in referring to Dora's first dream will be to compare the three theoretical models' current outlooks on adolescents' character disturbance.

In a 1900 letter to Fliess, Freud (1950) first mentioned Dora as an adolescent patient whose analysis had opened smoothly, but the case study was not published until 1905. Dora had first consulted Freud when she was sixteen years old, and she later agreed to begin her analysis, when she was eighteen at the urging of her father who was one of Freud's former patients. Dora had left a suicide note which her parents found. At the start of her analysis, she reported numerous conversion symptoms, such as dizziness, headaches, aphonia, coughing and neuralgia. Dora's overall presentation was that of an hysteric. Freud's etiological explanation for her symptoms contained his axiom that hysterical symptoms represented repressed, conflictual fantasies of sexual activity. A later account of Dora indicated that her analysis did not result in either long lasting symptomatic relief or characterological change. Felix Deutsch (1957) briefly treated Dora as an adult. In a far from felicitous statement of her mental status, Deutsch reported a description of the forty year old Dora as a "most repulsive" hysteric. In Freud's (1905) postscript to the case, he determined that the treatment failure - Dora's abrupt termination - took place because of his failure to quickly interpret the Oedipal transference, and his failure to recognize homosexual elements in the transference. A number of important essays about Dora have yielded alternate Freudian and interpersonal explanations for both her precipitous flight from therapy and its limited efficacy (Blos, 1972; Erikson, 1962; Kanzer, 1980; Glenn, 1980; Levenson, 1981; Marcus, 1974; Muslin and Gill, 1978; Rogow, 1978).

Current assessments of Dora's personality might begin with the surface manifestations of her hysterical character style, namely her compensatory self-dramatization, her global, impressionistic thinking and the immersion of her conflicts and repressed emotionality in her conversion symptoms. From our contemporary perspective, these tendencies would be understood as defensive expressions of failures in adolescent development. They would likewise be seen as the result of the internalization of destructive patterns of family relationships which were unknowingly recreated in the analytic relationship. Further analysis might reveal Dora's longstanding anxieties and affective configurations involving betrayal, self-hatred, the fear of annihilation and unconscious surrender to the experience of exploitation. The transference-countertransference exchanges would need to be investigated along these dynamic lines by clinicians of each psychoanalytic orientation. The ensuing observations will follow the outline of Freudian, interpersonal and object relations responses to the clinical material.

Dora's first dream was reported as follows:

> A house was on fire. My father was standing be sides my bed and woke me up. I dressed quickly. Mother wanted to stop and save her jewel case, but father said: I refuse to let myself and my two children be burnt for the sake of your jewel case. (Freud, 1905B)

The essence of the dream was interpreted to be Dora's repudiation of repressed sexual excitement at being kissed by her father's friend, Herr K. Herr K. had tried to seduce Dora when she was fourteen. The dream was a recurrent one which began when Dora was sixteen, after Herr K. proposed to her, and she felt indignant and frightened of further seduction. In addition, Dora's attacks of hysterical coughing and nervous asthma were considered by Freud to be both the result of sexual guilt and the equivalent of an unconscious fellatio fantasy. This fantasy was said to represent Dora's wish for sexual contact with her father, by means of identifying herself with Frau K. with whom her father had a longstanding affair. Dora's unconscious sexual longings for Herr K., and for her father, as well as her repressed homosexual feelings were depicted as the basis for the atmosphere of psychic danger which pervaded the dream. Freud did not connect the dream either with Dora's suicide note, which had first brought her to treatment, or with her likely feelings of betrayal, self-hatred and abandonment. His deduction was that Dora's clinical symptomatology emerged from her hysterical renunciation of the seducer, her own sexual excitation, and her repressed Oedipal wishes. Such factors as the parents' hypocrisy, the 19th century Viennese cultural attitudes towards women, and the influence of unrecognized countertransference hostility were beyond the realm of Freud's analysis of the transference and resistance.

Dora's feelings of outrage and her provocativeness were no doubt fueled by her lack of individuation and her betrayal by both of her parents. Dora had been betrayed by her parents' disbelief of her account of Herr K.'s sexual advances. Neither parent acknowledged Dora's father's offering her to Herr K., as compensation for his own affair with Frau K. Freud recognized, but made no mention of, the impact on Dora of the family's pretense and hypocrisy. If the reproach in the dream referred to Dora's feelings in addition to those of her father, then it signified her anger at her father's manipulativeness and dishonesty. The reproach in the dream simultaneously conveyed an attack on Freud, for his exposure of Dora's sexual secrets, at the expense of not validating her potentially painful insights into the family secrets. According to Freud's dream theory, the ties between manifest dream symbols and unconscious sexual wishes were repressed, because of the dangers of childhood sexual impulses and moral inhibitions. Dora's anxiety, and fury, about the possibility of betrayal in the transference-countertransference might have also been repressed. Dora's dream took place following Freud's interpretative statements about her autoerotic stimulation. Dora may have thus needed to retaliate for the frustration of her wish for validation, and encouragement, to use both herself, and the transference, in order to overcome her self-destructiveness and her attention seeking conversion symptoms. The dramatic presentation of Dora's father, as the heroic rescuer in the dream, hinted at Dora's ambivalence about an idealized father, as well as the provocativeness and narcissism which were presented to her as a model for identification. Finally, the father's appearance, in the dream, at the undressed Dora's bedside in the (passionate) heat of the fire pointed to the possible question of the seductiveness of both her father and Herr K. These speculative assumptions are lent some support by adolescents' tendency to include in their dreams, either a friend, or some other figure whose attitudes document the dreamer's self experience and inner reality.

Present day Freudian analysts would examine the effects of the family enmeshment on Dora's unconscious fantasies, in addition to the links between her somatic symptoms and the feelings in her internalized relationships. Dora's ego ideal, her sense of identity, her problems with individuation and deidealization, her unconscious need to mother her own body, and the secondary gains of her remaining the Oedipal child, would all be investigated. Anna Freud (1980) believed that the key to forming a therapeutic alliance with adolescent patients lay in helping the adolescent come to terms with the presence of some painful inner state which the analysis would address. Muslin and Gill (1978) pointed out that Freud's countertransference responses repeatedly interfered with his seeing transference references throughout the analysis. Blos (1972) formulated a number of critisms of Freud's interpretations of Dora's sexual wishes. He indicated that Dora's incipient neurotic character was crystallized by the analysis which treated her as though she were an adult who had achieved psychic separation from the family. In an observation, with which most psychoanalysts would agree, Blos argued that poorly timed id interpretations will be heard by adolescents as parental seductions. Freud's interpretations about Dora's masturbatory conflicts, and her repressed wishes for sexual contact with both himself and her father, could have been heard as a seductive enticement. In a final criticism of Freud's handling of Dora, Erikson (1962) distinguished the role of psychological reality from the importance of historical actuality. Freud dismissed both the seriousness of Dora's interest in analysis and her request for validation of her perceptions. For Erikson, Freud's double failure consisted of his ignoring Dora's developmental considerations, and his not understanding that adolescent patients genuinely need validation of historical actuality.

Interpersonal and Object Relations
Aspects of Dora

From Sullivan's point of view, an adolescent patient, like Dora, would have needed to give up private disordered experience, during analysis, by making use of consensual validation. On the basis of the analyst's participant observation, the therapeutic cure for adolescents occurred through the elimination of dissociation and the newfound possibility of profiting from present and future life experience. As a telling comment on Erikson's comment, Levenson (1981) called into question Freud's assumption that patients' fantasies constituted the primary data of psychoanalytic inquiry. In interpersonal theory, transference-countertransference transactions have long been considered to be a continuous process of mutual influence. Freud's neglect of Dora's seduction by her family, and his overall neglect of other interpersonal issues, has been scrutinized by Slipp (1977), Spiegel (1977), and other authors.

Speculation about the origins of Freud's negative countertransference with Dora has in no way detracted from the momentous historical value of this fragmentary analysis. Gay's (1988) authoritative biography of Freud implied that several key relationships in Freud's life might have united the disparate elements of his countertransference feelings towards his female patients. Gay hypothesized that the adolescent Freud's unrequited love for his friend's sister, Gisela Fluss, unleashed highly impassioned psychic forces. In addition, Freud's emotional overinvolvement with his oldest daughter was reported, by Gay, to have, on occasion, reached an extreme intensity. At the time of Dora's analytic sessions with Freud, in 1900, Anna Freud would have been approximately five years old and in the throes of the Oedipal conflict. Rogow (1978) believed that Dora was really Ida Bauer, the sister of a well known Marxist, socialist Austrian political leader. However, Kanzer's (1980) investigative efforts yielded the conclusion that Dora's real name was Rosa, the name of Freud's most cherished sister, and also the name of his sister's nursemaid. If Freud unconsciously identified Dora with any of these women, then Dora's analysis might have assembled his detachment and his hostility as defenses against his own unresolved Oedipal longings. With the transposition of Dora's analysis to the present, the analyst would not be exempt from considering all potential sources of countertransference influence on resistance and transference. A contemporary interpersonal analysis of Dora's dream would thus include Dora's possible recognition of her father's seductiveness, as well as her recognition of, and contribution to, Freud's unwitting recreation of her father's condescending exploitativeness.

From an interpersonal, object relations point of view, my own reading of Dora's first dream would emphasize the exploration of her most disturbing anxieties about annihilation, fusion and aggression. According to Kleinian theory, Dora's masturbation fantasies could not have escaped either the powerful influence of the death instinct, or her infantile conflicts with part-objects. These fantasies would be heard as an arena for her bellicose impulses and anxieties. If Dora associated the jewel case in the dream with her mother and herself, rather than her genitals, then the dream might have expressed the death anxiety which was connected with her fear of separation and her wish for the internalized good mother. Dora's repressed masturbation fantasies and sexual wishes could have therefore suggested a retreat from her terror of individuation, as well as the fear of her own rage projected onto the devouring penis and the annihilating breast. Furthermore, if Freud identified Dora with his sister's servant, then this dream might have also expressed the danger inherent in both his wish to be served and her enactment of her unconscious self image of being submissive to exploitation.   A contemporary analysis of Dora would necessitate her experiencing and relinquishing such affective connections between the frantic, devalued, victimized self and the object as the seductive, hostile agent of betrayal. The theme of seduction and betrayal would need to be explored as it unfolded in the analytic relationship.

In his extension of Klein's ideas, Fairbairn accounted for hysterical character trends, like Dora's, as recreations in the genital sphere of earlier oral problems. He maintained that Freud's polarization of libido and aggression was a false dichotomy, because feelings of hate lay in readiness beneath all intense dysphoric emotions. According to Winnicott's terminology, an adolescent analysand, like Dora, would need to ruthlessly demand a new maternal object in order to fully prosper in relating. At the very least, Dora would be presented with the ambience of, what Winnicott considered to be an optimal environment for facilitating her genuine self's return, from dissociation. What would have been of great concern (for Fairbairn) was the absorption of Dora's wish for her father's penis into her need for his emotional availability, and (for Sullivan) the effect of this unsatisfied need on Dora's self-esteem and interpersonal inference making.   In harmonious accordance with the current Freudian and interpersonal models of clinical practice, an object relations approach to Dora's dreams would use the transference-countertransference transactions as a potential source of understanding of both her psychic state and the therapeutic interaction.

Conclusion

The Freudian, interpersonal and object relations theories of treatment have suggested different starting points for the investigation of adolescents' characterological problems.   Nevertheless, present day analysts, of all orientations, would be compelled to investigate Dora's relationship with her body as a vehicle for her object relationships, her internalized rage and her other dissociated affects. My references to these three theoretical models, and their clinical implications, have focused on adolescence.   Overall comparisons of the psychoanalytic models of metapsychology have been offered by Guntrip (1961), Greenberg and Mitchell (1983), Kwawer (1981), Ticho (1978) and others.   These authors provided comprehensive critiques of the similarities and differences between classical theory, Sullivan's theory and object relations theories.   Each of the theoretical models of adolescent maturation, which I have discussed, established the conceptual connections between problems in adolescent development, and the emergence of psychopathology, but they did so from different directions. Freudian theorists emphasized the integration of the drives and defenses in the libidinal fixations and the structural changes of adolescence. In Sullivan's pragmatic, but hopeful, vision of personality development, the self system, which included character, reduced the adolescent to a diminished caricature of what he or she might have become.   In Winnicott's, optimistic theory of development, some degree of insanity was necessary for the adolescent's optimal adjustment.   Winnicott claimed that this measure of madness was essential, if the adolescent was to avoid sacrificing individuality in light of the need to remain unknown, by adults, yet authenticly alive.   Interpersonal and object relations theories of development highlighted cultural forces, dissociative processes and the disruptive anxieties inherent in adolescents' self-object dialogues.

CHAPTER THREE

Abusive Families and Character Formation

I feel bad because I am bad. I am bad because she does not love me.
She does not love me because I am bad.

R.D. Laing

There has been little evidence of a one to one correspondence between specific forms of child abuse and later psychopathology. However, many clinical reports of abused children and adolescents have pointed to ego impairments, extreme dissociation and regressive defenses as the aftereffects of abuse in addition to the damage to the child's self. By commenting, in this chapter, on abusive families' interactions, I will draw attention to the role of family processes in the development of depressive, paranoid and borderline character features.

At the risk of overgeneralizing on the basis of limited data, I will draw inferences from the treatment of adolescents and children who have been physically, sexually, and emotionally abused. My aim will be descriptive, rather than diagnostic, in bringing to light the impact of abusive family interactions on adolescents' defensive processes and emerging character trends. Emotional or psychological abuse is comprised of recurrent critical attacks in which both the child's emerging self and the child's individuation is contemptuously devalued. Like physical abuse and sexual abuse, severe psychological abuse forces the child or adolescent to defend against mourning and dependency needs. As one type of trauma, abuse fosters the extensive use of denial and dissociation in order for the youth to avoid mourning and possible fragmentation. Unlike other types of trauma, in which the child is able to identify with or rely on the parents for support and ego augmentation, the abused youngster tends to internalize the abusive family atmosphere while experiencing the loss of the good parent and the good self.

Like physically and sexually abusive parents, psychologically abusive families contribute to the development of paranoid, depressive and borderline character traits which become more apparent during middle and late adolescence. The emotional impact of severe psychological abuse initially arises in family transactions which curb the child's ego development and perpetuate hostile, regressed types of relatedness. Empirical studies have documented the incidence of depressive self-hatred and disassociation in sexually abused children, and antisocial conduct in physically abused children. Abused youngsters, in general, encounter difficulty in negotiating the tasks of adolescence and in resolving the depressions which stem from guilt, shame, neglect, rage, experiences of loss, and the internalization of belittlement.

Abuse and Trauma

In psychoanalytic theory, abuse has been assessed from the point of view of trauma, and trauma has been considered to be a crucial organizer of psychic life. Each of the three psychoanalytic theoretical models, has depicted the importance of traumatic experience as an unconscious organizing principle. Beginning with Freud's (1926) formulations about trauma and the stimulus barrier of excitation, psychoanalytic theorists have noted the deleterious effects of traumatic situations. Even though Freud gave up his seduction theory of neurosis, the classical Freudian model emphasized trauma's negative effects on the ego. Anna Freud (1967) amplified this concept of trauma as an organizing force which shaped ego and character development. She believed that trauma disrupted developmental processes, because it contributed to both general ego impairment and the ego's helplessness. In a forerunner of the interpersonal psychoanalytic model, which was couched in Freudian terminology, Ferenczi (1932) observed the sexually abused child's self-hate, fragmentation and impaired ability to trust and to love. In a prelude to contemporary interest in internalized object relations, Ferenczi stressed the abused child's internalization of both the abuse and the abuser along with the inner sense of badness. Fairbairn's (1952) descriptions of splitting within the ego explained how traumatized children identify with dissociated aspects of their parents. All forms of abuse mold the child's identifications and interpersonal enactments of conflict, including the enactments of object relations patterns in transference-countertransference exchanges. Abused patients' interactions fully illustrate the central dynamic importance of Freud's concept of the repetition-compulsion.

Psychological Abuse and Mourning

Psychological abuse can best be described as the parental acting out of unconscious hatred and dependency, facilitated by means of the sadistic use of projective processes. For all types of abused children, the abuse leads to denial and constriction of the experiencing self. Abuse stimulates heightened anxiety about mastering developmental tasks and attaining differentiation from the internal objects. As a foundation for character development, the abused child's felt experience often includes not only desertion, humiliation, rage, guilt, shame and self-loathing, but also confusion about both interpersonal meaning and inner reality.

When Sullivan (1956) made a distinction between normal and pathological grief, he characterized the latter as the absence of mourning whereby an overwhelming loss stops the "erasing function" of the self. The abused child or adolescent maintains a defensive struggle to avoid mourning. Abused youngsters' depressive orientation evolves from a combination of this struggle with the devaluation inherent in parental attacks and their multiple experiences of loss. Their difficult losses include the abrupt loss of the idealized parent, the idealized self, the loss of security, the loss of parental empathy at key points in development, and finally the loss of developmentally appropriate emotional, cognitive and social skills.

Abused children and adolescents' sense of helplessness and their confusion about meaning adds to their difficulties in sustaining relatedness in other than paranoid or depressive modes. Poorly integrated, psychologically abused youngsters' lack of anxiety tolerance fosters their impulsive and, at times, provocative behavior. When they feel threatened, abusive parents attack their children's self-esteem, while encouraging regression and discouraging age-appropriate functioning.

An explosive, vividly troubled fifteen year old adolescent girl, who stole from her family and had temper outbursts during which she physically attacked her younger siblings, had the following hate-filled conversation with her parents. Mother: "I wish you were never born. You're going to be a dropout and a drug addict." Daughter: "I hate your guts. You're evil. I wish I was adopted." Father: (Silence).

The mother's constant condemnations and the father's passivity and withdrawal were equally hurtful to this girl during family screaming matches.   The rage and the hateful threats inherent in this family's dialogues underscored their lack of differentiation and their sadistic use of projective processes.   Abusive parents frequently attack when they misperceive a child's problems as damaging criticisms.   Abusive parents' failures in empathy give way to rage when their child or adolescent fails to meet what may be unrealistic expectations.   Severely abused children's internalization of such interactions, and their defenses against primitive anxiety and mourning, remain important bases for the self and character.

Defensive Processes and Character Trends

During adolescence, characterological defenses become increasingly organized in order to ward off the death or annihilation anxiety inherent in abusive family relationships, as the adolescent's perceptions of his or her own basic needs and thought processes come under attack in the family.   Youngsters from highly abusive families exhibit not only depression and cognitive deficits, such as poor abstraction ability, but also limitations in self-awareness and problems with the identification and differentiation of feelings (Green, 1981).   Many severely abused adolescents reveal a paranoid-like hypersensitivity, and distortions of interpersonal transactions, which evolve into the adult paranoid's suspiciousness and manipulativeness.   Splitting and dissociation serve as vigorous, if not primary, defenses against the loss of the self and the object.

The connections between depression and paranoia, and between paranoia and borderline traits, constituted early themes in psychoanalytic theory.   More recently, these dynamic and characterological ties have been traced to the aftereffects of abusive family relationships.   Klein (1948) stressed the connection between depression and paranoia in infantile fantasies, after Freud noted the link between depression and the paranoid's projection of self-hatred.   There is some similarity between the idea that abusive families continually attack the self and Sullivan's (1956) concept of malevolent transformation in relation to parental hostile integration.   Current research on abusive family systems is also congruent with Winnicott's (1947) recounting of childhood feelings of hate and maturational failures which occur in the course of lapses in the early environment.   Bonime (1982) discussed many characterological similarities between the depressive and the paranoid, including their hostility, covert demandingness, and hypersensitivity. Guntrip (1969) observed that the schizoid defense allows for escape from persecutory anxiety and depressive anxiety, which are both object-relational experiences. Meissner (1978) argued that the tie between depression and paranoia is so close that the giving up of the paranoid character style can occur in treatment only at the risk of experiencing severe depression. His position has been that the same abusive family interactions which lead to depression also lead to paranoid character traits.

Abusive families stimulate the widespread use of dissociation and denial, while fostering the repetition compulsion of abusive attacks against the self and others. Such families have in common systems of functioning which simultaneously rely on hostile attacks and dependence on the adolescent as an outlet for the parents' unsatisfied needs and damaged self-esteem (Helfer and Kempe, 1987). The abusive family environment inflicts further damage by reinforcing the massive use of repression, instead of facilitating the youth's growing relatedness and self-awareness. Sexual, physical and severe psychological abuse all curb emotional development, both by defining intimacy in terms of abusive interactions, and by interfering with the processing of affective states which are too anxiety-provoking to be integrated (Finkelhor, 1984; Furst, 1967; Krystal, 1978).

Although not all abused youngsters develop either paranoid or borderline psychopathology, the abusive family system fosters borderline and paranoid defensive processes along with depression and distortions of reality. The denial of reality and splitting remains a frequent aspect of family transactions which envelop the child in sadistic family bonds. The perceptual and conceptual world of severely abused children and adolescents relies on dissociation in order to maintain an avoidance of awareness of exploitation in the family. Impairments in reality testing and disturbances in the sense of reality are not uncommon among very severely abused latency age children and adolescents.

The adolescent patient I mentioned earlier related a frightening dream. In the dream, she attended a church service in which the minister conducted a devil worship ceremony for the members of a satanic cult. At its conclusion, an eight or nine year old girl was tortured and mutilated on the altar. In the midst of her associations, the

patient reflected on her memory of an imaginery friend who
had kept her company when she was around eight years old.
The companion, Sandy, had soothed and comforted her during
periods of intense loneliness. By the time of the dream, Sandy
had become a fully dissociated self and a delusional presence
whose critical voice persecuted the patient for her inadequacies
and her sexual fantasies about her classmates. With little
defensive disguise the dream succinctly recorded her ego
splitting, her rage and her self- persecution. The dream's
latent content conveyed with relish the complementary
annihilation and Oedipal anxieties which haunted this girl's
fantasies and the transference. What initially struck me about
the dream was the diabolical sterility of the family atmosphere
and the early origins of the patient's dissociative processes and
self-hate.   When I asked the patient to consider how our
relationship was like torture, for her, her feeling of rage and
fears of annihilation became more available. This gradual
recognition helped to improve her reality testing.

The Schreber case (Freud, 1911) illustrated that the internalization of
abuse can account for paranoid, psychotic elaborations of what were
originally appropriate signs of mistrust and ideas of reference.   The
abused youth's paranoid reliance on projection and narrowing of the
perceptual field makes sense as a judicious defensive response. Abused
adolescents' waves of rage, and their ambivalent attachments to their
families, coexist with defensive confusion about the nature of their
perceptions and the interpersonal impact of others.

Abusive parent-child interactions thwart adolescents' increasing grasp
of inner reality and their developmental progress in resolving age-related
tasks.   Their comprehension of interpersonal events is slanted by
character organization which is flooded by anxiety and depressive affects.
Abusive parents typically select one particular child as the target for their
use of projection and projective identification. The repetitive use of early
projective processes provides a model for reliance on these defenses by
the abused child. Abusive parents also strongly depend on their children
when they feel anxious or devalued, and they attack the children at points
of their own frustration and the child's individuation. Feelings of envy
and rage contribute to the mutual provocations which take place with the
physically and psychologically abused school-aged child or adolescent.

The adolescent child's part in this hostile dialogue often consists of engaging in impulsive, destructive and self-destructive behavior in order to confirm the parents' projections and to avoid mourning and further anxiety about loss. The parents unconsciously identify the adolescent with their own abusive parents, against whom they are retaliating, or with themselves as they recreate family dramas of deprivation and abuse.

Family communications characterized by belittlement and humiliation provide a model for the adolescent depressive's self-criticisms, just as they contribute to making failure and incompetence primary qualities of the child's reflected appraisals. The loss of the good or idealized parent and the good self is abrupt in abusive families, rather than a gradual relinquishment of images that provide security. The constant sense of failure to gratify parents' expectations further adds to the abused adolescent's depressive character orientation. Not only the emergence of the self, but also emotional integration is inhibited by the abusive family system.

Abusive parents have in common an unempathic overidentification with the child and the consistent use of the child to counterbalance their own projections and disappointments. When severely disturbed parents feel threatened, they may abuse their child in order to eradicate the child's ego boundaries and signs of the child's self. Because of parental distortions that all types of abuse are for the child's own good, abusive families help create a paranoid hypervigilence and hypersensitivity to hostility. The adolescent's need for differentiation from a positive parental image contributes to his or her confusion about interpersonal meaning and misinterpretation of hostile interactions. Abused adolescents' shame and anxiety adds to their difficulty in sustaining healthy ego states and their lack of flexibility in defensive operations. As their parents devalue them by attacking them physically, sexually, and psychologically, they often withdraw into the family rather than take advantage of emotional opportunities for reparation provided by peers or by substitute parent figures. Their heavy reliance on dissociation, repression, splitting and denial hinders the developmental demands of healthy character consolidation.

Abuse and Adolescent Character Consolidation

As a result of their self-hate, their confusion and their internalization of the abuse, severely abused adolescents are at great risk for interrupted individuation. They likewise tend to be subject to great difficulty with the adolescent predicaments of intimacy and sexuality. According to Shengold (1989), victims of severe physical and sexual abuse during childhood must somehow integrate the most inconceivably traumatic affects. Shengold hypothesized that a hypnotic vigilance defends them against both drive discharge and the onset of further abuse. Sexually abused adolescents experience massive problems with self representations in addition to their subsequent difficulties with their own sexuality (Margolis, 1984; Obrien, 1987). My experience with severely disturbed, physically and sexually abused adolescents has suggested the prevalence of their cognitive deficits and severe gaps in their ego functioning. The common denominators of these patients' clinical features have included extreme emotional lability, concrete thinking and deficits in symbolic fantasy. Many have exhibited an inability to differentiate feeling states, along with a projection of rage in which almost any frustration of their wishes is experienced as an abusive persecution. Retrospective experimental studies of young adults, who have been diagnosed as having a borderline personality disorder, have suggested a relationship between borderline features and childhood histories of physical and sexual abuse (Herman, Perry, van der-Kolk, 1989; Stone, 1990). The derailment of abused individuals' emotional and psychological maturation extends to their internalization of abuse as a foundation for character formation.

Abusive families counteract the evolution of the abused child's self whether the self is viewed in phenomenological, systemic, or intrapsychic terms. Definitions of the self in theory have included its description as the integrated whole of the person, a system of reflected appraisals, a system of organizing tendencies that shapes experience, and an inclusive term for unique internal processes which include the ego and identity. By employing denigrations, and physical or sexual domination, abusive families' attacks resonate with the child's deepest fears about individuation or the survival of the self and the object. However, with the exception of sexual abuse and severe physical abuse, a single traumatic event seldom definitively molds character consolidation. Yet, as an organizer of infantile anxieties, any trauma effects both antecedent conflict and those of later developmental stages (Kennedy, 1986).

During childhood and adolescence, repetitive family interactions tend to be symbolized as family dramas. Traumatic events, such as sexual abuse, or verbal and physical explosions of parental hatred, emotionally color one's experience of the self and others. They contribute to the amount of distortion in the abused child or adolescent's transferential relationships, just as they give rise to fantasies about being deserving of the abuse.

The adolescent or young adult who was an abused child maintains defenses against remembering and trusting, as well as against being involved in new experience. Both the abused individual who acts out, and the one who internalize hate, recoils from intimacy, since intimacy has signified being attacked and humiliated in the family. The need to repeat the abuse and to cling to the internalized abusive family extends beyond identification with the aggressor. The unconscious roles of victim, abuser, and heroic rescuer may be recreated in intimate relationships and in the transference during psychoanalytic treatment.

A paranoid worldview, flight from emotional contact and defenses against feelings of helplessness and worthlessness, thus unfold in the analytic relationship with the abused adolescent or adult. During adolescence, the transformation of the abused into the abuser continues intrapsychically, and as a product of family interactions which continue the abuse. As the victimized youth gradually becomes the adult abuser, repetitive attacks are directed against the self and the internalized objects. The analytic experienc for such patients proceeds with the unconscious assumption that intimacy will entail exploitation and devaluation. The use of the analytic process allows the patient to acknowledge massive repression, and dissociation, as well as the translation of abusive family experience into destructive emotional patterns.

Child and adolescent clinicians observe at close hand unhealthy characterological changes which escalate as abusive families thwart healthy individuation. Psychoanalysts often become aware of an adolescent or a young adult's history of being abused by means of feelings of hate and sexual arousal in the transference-countertransference, in addition to the patient's use of dissociation. Feelings of hate in the transference-countertransference signal the continuance of unconscious attacks against the patient's self, the internalized family, and the analyst. Provocative or self-destructive actions may also accompany these patients' trenchant defenses against the anticipation of sexual betrayal, or exploitation and abandonment in the analytic relationship.

Ferenczi (1932) first described these phenomena as the result of the abused child's anxiety-ridden identification with the aggressor and introjection of the aggressor's guilt feelings.   Reliving traumatic memories of abuse, during analysis, helps patients become free of those defenses and object relations patterns which are embedded in their prevailing character trends.

Conclusion

Family research studies have confirmed that abusive parents are undifferentiated partners who compete with each other and with their offspring for attention and nurturance.   More or less healthy parents make demands on their children to counteract their own injured narcissism, but they do so largely without devaluation and the sadistic use of projective identification.   Under sufficient stress, abusive parents attack the youth who fails to gratify their needs, thereby giving vent to longstanding frustrations and feelings of being threatened by the child's individuation and competency.   The emotional atmosphere in such families facilitates ego deficits like those of the borderline personality, as it molds the child's efforts to avoid the anxieties of a painful reality.

Devaluation, loss, and defenses against mourning partially account for abused youngsters' depressive and paranoid traits which are consolidated into dominant trends during middle and late adolescence.   Early neglect and abuse exposes them to influential models who act out rage and primitive defenses.   Some severely abused adolescents project their rage and later become paranoid or antisocial, whereas others fragment or retain infantile defenses.   Abusive family systems reinforce both interactional patterns of abuse and the child's reliance on early intrapsychic processes for dealing with attacks on the body and the self. Unhealthy character traits continue defensive processes which derive from the internalization of abuse and the compulsion to repeat abusive relationships.   Achieving individuation under these circumstances entails overcoming the internalized abusive relationships and relinquishing the unconscious wish to be transformed from abused into the abuser.

PART II

PRIMITIVE ANXIETY, CHARACTER, AND THE THERAPEUTIC PROCESS

CHAPTER FOUR

Death Anxiety and Character Disturbance

What Freud describes under the category of death instincts would thus appear to represent for the most part masochistic relationships with internalized bad objects.

W.R. Fairbairn

The life-destructive forces in a person occur in an inverse ratio to the life-furthering ones.

Eric Fromm

On the basis of Fromm's ideas, as well as those of Fairbairn, the fundamental relationship between separation anxiety, depression, and death anxiety has been said to persist in its psychodynamic interplay in personality functioning throughout human life (McCarthy, 1980). In this chapter, I will review this proposal concerning anxiety about annihilation which bridged the gap between the neurotic person's fear of death, and the more disturbed person's experience of primitive anxiety and inner disorganization. My primary purpose will be to compare Freudian, interpersonal and object relations views of death anxiety, and to discuss some of the pertinent theoretical contributions of Freud, Anna Freud, Klein, Fairbairn, Little and Fromm. I also wish to summarize psychoanalytic accounts of death anxiety's influence in neurotic trends, schizophrenic episodes and schizoid states. The term, death anxiety, has most often been used in psychoanalytic theory to refer to one aspect of primitive anxiety. A number of theorists have equated the concept of death anxiety with the continuum of annihilation fears, which range from neurotic separation fears and depression, to more disruptive, diffuse anxiety about disintegration of the self and the ego.

Introduction

The fear of death, in the physically healthy person, can be most clearly understood on several concurrent levels of psychological meaning. For the neurotic, death anxiety represents individuation difficulties inherent in depression and emotional constriction. For individuals with schizoid, borderline, narcissistic, antisocial, and other types of severe character disturbance, death anxiety registers a similar, but more pervasive, fierce anxiety about utter annihilation and dissolution of the personality. As a stimulus for defensive operations, death anxiety influences character traits in formation, and it arises in psychoanalytic treatment at points of internal psychological separation as well as in resistance.

As an extension of interpersonal and object relations theories of character, it can be argued that, during adolescence, depression and failures in psychic separation increasingly express the death anxiety which is inherent in neurotic living. In addition, death anxiety constitutes both a symptom and a defense against disruptive, archaic affects which arise in analysis as the self attempts growth. The dynamic interplay between death anxiety, depression, and separation anxiety illustrates the existential notion of distorted purpose in life as the central core problem of character pathology (Frankl, 1962; Laing, 1960). My concept of death anxiety concertized Fromm's (1941) view of the neurotic fear of death as being synonymous with the fear of life, and hence the fear of freedom. It was also consonant with Fairbairn's idea that neurotic character organization expressed defenses against underlying primitive anxiety. Death anxiety has served as a major explanatory concept in each of the psychoanalytic models of character formation.

From different theoretical points of view, each psychoanalytic orientation has offered the supposition that death anxiety provides dynamic and developmental influences on character consolidation. From an interpersonal perspective, Schachtel's (1959) term, embeddedness, aptly described the experience of the self, without mature differentiation, which the neurotic, like the adolescent, grapples with in trying to arrive at self-definition and autonomy. The myth of Prometheus and the Biblical tale of Jonah provided abundant examples of this motif of the struggle of the embedded self for autonomy. The Freudian and object relations conceptions of death anxiety's formative influence originated with Freud's theory of the death instinct. Freud's concept of death

anxiety was later expanded in the object relations approaches of Klein, Fairbairn and Winnicott, while the neoFreudian, interpersonal theorists stressed the motivational power of death fears in neurotic character organization. Clinically, anxieties about death and annihilation need to be examined in all of their dimensions in relation to experienced threats to the self and the object. Self and object images involving death imagery, and fears of disintegration and annihilation are routinely uncovered in analytic work with patients of varying degrees of disturbance.

Death Anxiety in Freudian Theory

Any historical summary of the concept of death anxiety must begin with a review of Freud's genetic and topographic ideas about the death instinct. His theory of the death instinct remained one of the most controversial aspects of his metapsychology. As Freud's views on anxiety evolved, he came to distinguish traumatic anxiety from signal anxiety, and he placed a high degree of emphasis on the ego's sense of helplessness with overwhelming situations of external danger. However, in *Inhibitions Symptoms, and Anxiety,* Freud (1926) rejected the dynamic primacy of the fear of death, which he considered to be analogous to the fear of castration. According to Freud's theory, the biologically based death instinct was expressed in the ego as aggressive impulses. Freud (1923) concluded in *The Ego and the Id* that:

> the fear of death is something that occurs between the ego and the superego. We know that the fear of death makes its appearance under two conditions, namely, as a reaction to an external danger and as an internal process, as for instance in melancholia.... These considerations make it possible to regard the fear of death, like the fear of conscience, as a development of the fear of castration.

In a comprehensive review of Freud's death instinct theory, Chessick (1992) pointed out that the ambiguities of the definition of the death instinct prevented its widespread acceptance. With few exceptions, Freud seldom referred to the death instinct in his case studies, other than as diffuse instinctual aggression which was expressed destructively in sadism.

Among classical psychoanalysts, such as Fenichel and H. Deutsch,

neurotic death fears were attributed, in case material, to castration anxiety and to Oedipal guilt associated with sadistic and masochistic wishes. Fenichel (1953) was highly critical of the death instinct theory, which he saw as unwarranted, and as a completely biological explanation for neurosis. More contemporary Freudian theorists have stressed a fear of maternal destructiveness in the dynamics of death anxiety, in addition to the preOedipal connection between death fears and unrecognized or unanalyzed symbiotic needs (Rheingold, 1967; Stern, 1968). Klein (1935) threw light on the psychodynamic and developmental ties between death anxiety and depression, but she did so largely from the vantage point of infantile fantasies and libido theory, with little reference to the self. Fairbairn (1943) was the first theorist to substantially connect Freud's psychology of the death instinct with the establishment of truly internalized object relationships. The theoretical line, to which he held, showed the ego's capacity to control death anxiety as a derivation of object relationships. Following in Fairbairn's tradition, Kohut's (1977) self psychology perspective, attributed death anxiety to the feared loss of selfobject mirroring. Fairbairn, Fromm and the existential psychoanalytic theorists all devoted considerable attention to the impact of death fears on adults' neurotic character organization. However, Anna Freud and Melanie Klein provided the most carefully delineated descriptions of the development of death anxiety during childhood and adolescence.

In her essay on the fear of regression, Anna Freud (1952) linked death fears to unconscious threats to the intactness of the ego. Such threats consisted of the fear of disintegration of the personality, together with the fear of the loss of sanity and personal characteristics. In *Normality and Pathology in Childhood,* she postulated three different types of conflicts and corresponding anxieties during early development (A. Freud, 1965). In the first type, the pleasure principle dictated a union of ego and id in which infantile anxieties were stimulated by frustrations brought about by the external world. These anxieties followed a chronological sequence, beginning with the fear of annihilation due to the loss of the caretaking object, followed by the fear of loss of the object's love. Subsequent to this second course of anxiety, which was dependent upon the establishment of object constancy, anxieties about criticism and punishment became dominant during the anal sadistic stage. Finally, castration anxiety emerged as the main

anxiety during the phallic-Oedipal period. In the second and third type of anxiety, relatively internalized and exclusively internal conflicts predominated. Such internal conflicts referred to guilt, as well as anxieties about incompatible drives and affect representations. Anna Freud retained Freud's distinction between traumatic anxiety and signal anxiety by working out in detail the nature of traumatic anxiety states, which had initially been described in *Beyond the Pleasure Principle.* Anna Freud's main contributions to this area of theory were her chronological sequence of developmental anxieties and her discussion of the ego's incapacitation by fears of annihilation.

Death Anxiety in Object Relations Theories and Interpersonal Theory

Melanie Klein (1946, 1948) openly disagreed with Freud's decision to not consider death anxiety as one of the fundamental anxieties or situations of danger. As an extension of Freud's theory of the death instinct, Klein argued that the fear of annihilation was the cause of all anxieties. In an early paper on *Infant Analysis,* Klein (1923) elaborated on the centrality of anxiety. She believed that the different neuroses shielded the ego from the emergence of anxiety as a primary affect. According to Klein's theory, anxiety maintained its dominant role in the formation of the personality, because of aggression, not sexuality. The internalized parents, in Freud's concept of the superego, became the persecutory internal objects in Klein's theory. Based on Freud's paper *Economic Problems in Masochism,* Klein (1948) stated in *On the Theory of Anxiety and Guilt* that the threat of the fear of death amounted to the unconscious dangers posed by the internalized devouring mother and father. In Kleinian theory, the infant's ego was said to contain both devoured and devouring objects. These dangerous internalized objects represented the death instinct. The child's unconscious fear of being eaten was thus transformed into the dread of complete annihilation. Klein's theoretical position on death anxiety was partially endorsed, and expanded, by Guntrip and Fairbairn.

As an interpreter of Fairbairn's theory, Guntrip criticized Sullivan, and the other interpersonal theorists, for an insufficient emphasis on the disruptive intensity of the dangers of the internal world. Nevertheless, Sullivan's outline of the personifications in early development (the good-me, the bad-me, and the not-me) was somewhat similar to Fairbairn's vision of the self's needs for internalized objects. Like Fairbairn, Guntrip believed in the deepest infantile anxiety as the source of character pathology and ego defenses. Guntrip's (1961) account of schizoid or primitive anxiety continued Fairbairn's reasoning. Guntrip described the undercurrent of primitive anxiety in the personality as a reaction to disturbing figures' persecution of repressed portions of the ego. Fairbairn (1952) only partially accepted Klein's view of annihilation anxiety in his hypotheses about the antilibidinal ego and the neurotic character defenses.

Fairbairn disagreed with Klein by means of his suggestion that the bad object was internalized first, prior to the internalized good object. It was Fairbairn's belief that, as a result of splitting, the bad, destructive object was internalized in order for it to be mastered. He depicted the infant's antilibidinal efforts to eliminate the frustration of unsatisfied needs, as a turning of destructive energy against the self. The psychoneurotic character trends (obsessional, phobic, hysterical and paranoid) were, therefore, considered defensive strategies for dealing with the bad internalized objects. According to Fairbairn, these neurotic strategies allowed the ego to avoid depressed and schizoid states. For both Fairbairn and Guntrip, death fears and primitive anxieties were understood as expressions of the interpersonal world, as well as manifestations of relationships with internalized bad objects.

Winnicott's concept of death anxiety placed the mother and the early environment at the center of the unfolding of primitive anxieties. Insufficient gratification of infants' dependency needs presented threats to the continuity of the self, while infants' ego development stemmed from recovery from such threats of annihilation. In the paper, *Primary Maternal Preoccupation*, Winnicott (1956) summed up his position.

> Maternal failures produce phases of reaction to impingement and these reactions interrupt the 'going on being' of the infant. An excess of this reacting produces not frustration, but a threat of annihilation. This in my view is a very real primitive anxiety, long antedating an anxiety that includes the word death in its description.

Like Klein, Winnicott and Fairbairn each reduced the concept of castration anxiety to an explanation for essentially neurotic, less destabilizing death anxiety which did not threaten existence.

Margaret Little's writings on transference themes returned to the issue of the dread of annihilation in borderline and psychotic individuals. Her work attested to her own acute sensitivity to primitive anxieties and to the legacy of Winnicott's developmental theory. In contrast to neurotic patients who could take their existence and sense of personal identity for granted, Little reported that much more disturbed patients were fixated in a state of undifferentiation which rendered them vulnerable to the terror of psychic annihilation. In Little's (1981) view:

> The fear of annihilation...is dynamic and all-pervading and therefore governs the patient's reactions and his behavior, both in relation to the analyst and to his environment. This fear, and the drive to establish identity with the analyst, lead him both to avoid these states of depersonalization and undifferentiatedness and at the same time to seek them, at any cost to himself or to the analyst. By reason of the life-and-death quality of the patient's experiences...and the fact that events belonging to earliest infancy are being lived out in a grown-up body, these phases of the analysis contain a large element of actual danger (suicide, death, or attack upon someone, often the analyst), which calls for great care in the management of the case.

According to Little's theory, psychotic patients suffered from the illusion of the state of "undifferentiated basic unity". This state evoked annihilation anxiety which developmentally preceded (Klein's) persecutory anxiety. Such annihilation fears were rooted in separation anxieties about the loss of objects which were not perceived either as whole, or as distinctly separate. Little's identification of such annihilation anxiety paralleled Winnicott's (and A. Freud's) delineation of intense anxiety that threatened the ego with disintegration. The death anxiety theories, espoused by Fairbairn, Winnicott, and Little, were each buttressed by their discussions of the derailment of disturbed patients' ego maturation.

As I mentioned in Chapter Two, Erikson's theory of personality development established a bridge to both object relations theories and interpersonal theory. His concept of the fear of death revived the humanistic theory of Fromm and those of other interpersonal theorists. Erikson was impressed by the lack of maturity, and the loss of accrued adaptations, in adults who evidenced strong fears about death. In *Childhood and Society*, Erikson (1950) wrote that death anxiety signified the mature adult's lack of ego integrity and lost ability to nurture and care for others. The absence of such ego integrity indicated the loss of a postnarcissistic love of humanity and the ego. This serious note, which Erikson struck about mature character organization, reiterated Fromm's highlighting of productivity and altruism in the non-neurotic, mature, type of character orientation. In Fromm's writings, the physically healthy person's death fears were defined as the neurotic fear of the loss of the self, given credence by the inactivity and helplessness of the unindividuated self.

Interpersonal and existential personality theorists found in the fear of death the self's estrangement from healthy living and a significant impetus for defensive processes. Both Fairbairn's theory of primitive anxiety, and Winnicott's view of annihilation anxiety resembled Sullivan's description of dissociation and not-me experience in primitive anxiety. Sullivan's writings repeatedly addressed the fragmentation and isolation encountered in schizophrenic episodes. In an attempt to understand the disintegrative anxieties, to which the vulnerable adolescent is subject, he probed the dynamic forces beneath clinical phenomena. Speaking in his highly personal, circuitous style, Sullivan argued that death anxiety could provide a frame of reference for psychopathology. It was Sullivan's (1956) contention that severe disturbance marked:

> An almost unceasing fear of becoming an exceedingly unpleasant form of nothingness...

From an interpersonal vantagepoint, a dialectical view of psychopathology has been maintained, in which each symptomatic expression of neurosis or psychosis has been seen as a depiction of the struggle for psychic survival. In a similar vein, Singer (1970) defined resistance as a reflection of patients' erroneous belief in the necessity of neurotic operations for maintaining life and dignity. Binswanger, Becker (1973), and other existentialists, extended the centrality of death anxiety to the point of documenting unrecognized death fears as the cause of all psychological disturbance.

While object relations theorists have pointed to borderline, psychotic and schizoid patients' failures to surmount death anxiety, many interpersonal theorists have emphasized death fears as the neurotic outcome of depression and clinging to the infantile world. According to the premises of interpersonal theory, death fears can be assessed in relation to both the paralyzing terror of dissociated states and experienced

threats to security.   The theoretical and clinical papers of Klein
Fairbairn, Guntrip, Winnicott, and Little remained consistent in their
accounting of borderline, schizoid and psychotic patients' anxieties which
were more primitive than the discrete fear of death.   Many of these
issues have been taken up, elsewhere, in theoretical studies of neurotic
and psychotic psychopathology.   Thorough discussions of Freud's
theories of anxiety, and the Freudian theory of death anxiety, have been
offered by Comptom (1981), Guntrip (1961) and Hurvich (1992).
Interpersonal and object relations assessments of death anxiety's influence
on character development have also been provided by Fromm-Reichmann
(1959) and Balint (1968).

Death Anxiety and Neurosis

Fromm, Horney and Sullivan acclaimed that the juxtaposition of
primitive anxiety and character traits found full expression and a concise
lexicon in neurotic conflicts.   Fromm most forcefully described death
anxiety as an outgrowth of neurotic passivity and helplessness which
corresponded to the lack of psychic individuation.   The obvious
differences between a neurotic patient's transference expressions of death
anxiety, and those of schizophrenic or borderline patients, lies in that, in
the latter individuals, there is a much more complete loss of the self and
intactness of ego boundaries.   Neurotics' merger never becomes so
complete, nor are their boundaries so blurred, that they fully experience
the powerful dread of bodily disintegration and annihilation of the ego.
Furthermore, the neurotic's need for fusion with the analyst does not
disclose the same degree of persecutory affects, and terror of
annihilation, as does the psychotic or borderline patient's transference
regression.   The neurotic patient's transference fusion remains more
reversible, with less need for the analyst to augment the patient's ego
functioning.   The analytic work with a neurotic patient's death anxiety
has, as its goal, the analysis of character flaws, and distortions as they
relate to threats to the self.
The dynamic relationship between death anxiety and depression,
which Freud and Klein first proposed, becomes apparent in analysands'
neurotic difficulties with characterological change.   The fear of death, or
annihilation of the self and the object, is evoked by the task of mourning
internal objects.   The prospect of emotional change brings ambivalent
hopes about giving up the conflicts and defenses inherent in unconscious

attachments. Anxiety filled depressions accompany the unconscious fear of the loss of the self and the object. Fromm and Horney both suggested that this kind of neurotic resourcelessness reinforced depression, while intense death anxiety underscored depressed feelings of hopelessness and helplessness. Suicidal impulses, in some severe depressions, may thus be interpreted as involving a defensive flight from death anxiety, through a wish for the loss of the self. During the course of analytic treatment, death anxiety becomes manifest as an expression of depression, and also as a defense against depressive affects. Fromm's work carefully scrutinized this mutual fear of life and death, which entraps the neurotic individual in the life destructive forces of a non-productive character style.

Before discussing death anxiety in schizophrenic and schizoid character trends, I will first briefly summarize Fromm's ideas about death anxiety in neurotic character organization. Fromm (1947) observed, in *Man for Himself*, that a neurotic fear of death was manifest in the fear of adult relatedness and active productivity. Kierkegaard had first related this inner sense of despair and anxiety about non-being to a "sickness unto death". Many of Kafka's stories also symbolicly expressed the immobilizing depression, and neurotic passivity, which Fromm equated with the fear of death. In a discussion of Kafka's *The Trial*, Fromm (1951) related the protagonist, K's, death anxiety to a neurotic, receptive character orientation, in which the wish to receive dominated his personality. Fromm described K's incarceration as the result of a sterile, empty life without productive efforts or loving relatedness. K's terror of his own execution ultimately provided him with the possibility of authentic, productive living which was not governed by "arrested" development. According to Fromm, K's transformation, at the end of the story, symbolized victory over a neurotic level of death anxiety and alienation from the self. Neurotic character orientations evolved from such thwarted strivings for freedom and independence (Fromm, 1941). Fromm labelled neurotic defensive processes, the mechanisms of *Escape from Freedom*. Such mechanisms of escape fostered the neurotic avoidance of aloneness and anxiety about individuation. In a line of reasoning which was very similar to that of Horney (1950), Fromm argued that neurotic symptoms should be compared to authoritarian ideologies which dominate the person with absolute control. Neurotic character trends offered the means for submission to such authority. For Fromm, the unfortunate result of neurotic character trends was the loss of identity and the loss of freedom inherent in death anxiety.

Death Anxiety and Schizophrenia

Beginning with Freud's work on the psychoses, many psychoanalytic theorists have acknowledged the emergence of death anxiety in specific symptoms among patients with schizophrenic disorders (Eissler, 1951; Federn, 1952; Rosen, 1952). On the basis of his extensive experience in treating schizophrenics, Searles (1961, 1965) came to several conclusions about death anxiety's impact. He affirmed that the certainty of death amounted to one of the major sources of anxiety in schizophrenia. Furthermore, schizophrenic illness, in Searles's view, involved a principal defense against anxiety about death. Arieti (1955) and Fromm-Reichmann (1959), likewise, depicted the fear of death, and the fear of psychological death, as an immensely powerful source of anxiety for schizophrenics which directly led to their symptomatology. Sullivan emphasized the loneliness, and the helplessness, which was part of the basis for schizophrenics' bizarre symptoms and ideation. Schizophrenics remain subject to facing the Herculean task of coming to terms with death anxiety, without having been fully integrated. Social ineptitude and ego deficits reinforce schizophrenic patients' sense of helplessness in reconciling death's finality with the chance of healthy, actualized living. The fear of losing pieces of one's body, which signifies inner fragmentation, looms as a related source of primitive anxiety for schizophrenic patients. The self-mutilation of some schizophrenic and borderline patients seems comprehensible, in this context, as an expression of defensive attempts to minimize primary process anxiety about annihilation and depersonalization. Instances of self-mutilation and other self abusive behaviors may be directed at controlling death anxiety by enacting the experience of inner persecution. Underlying fears of nothingness and the disintegration of the self have been noted, by several authors, beneath schizophrenic patients' agitated anxiety and interpersonal impoverishment.

A clinical vignette will illustrate death anxiety's dynamic significance in schizophrenia, and its relevance to transference.

Ms. A, a twenty year old woman, who was gradually improving from a profoundly catatonic state, following a lengthy hospitalization, reported the recovery of her earliest memory. Prior to the time she was able to walk, she remembered that she had been momentarily left on the street in her baby carriage. Although her memory lacked subtlety, and a richness of detail, she remembered looking up at the sight of a huge, vicious dog, growling at her, and baring its fangs. The abject terror of that instant was freed from repression, along with her conviction that she could have been killed and eaten by the hungry dog. There was no reason to doubt the psychological truthfulness of her report which became clear in the sessions.

Whether screen memory, fact or fantasy, this memory suggested an affective component of her inner experience, at least as she needed to reconstruct it.

At a point when the very young Ms. A. had been unable to flee from danger under her own power, a brief separation had suggested the prospect of total annihilation and absolute helplessness. During her childhood and adolescence, the developmental progression of her psychotic symptoms had insured protection from any such malevolent force, whether external and real, or internal and projected. Her catatonic regression had orchestrated the elements of a silent, motionless state of withdrawal in which no foreign element could possibly intrude and threaten her with annihilation. Ms. A's memory focused our attention on the survival function of her schizophrenic symptoms, as well as the connection between the fear of being eaten and the fear of fusion and annihilation. It recalled Sullivan's view of the schizophrenic's cosmic anxiety and need to flee from psychological danger. My references to interpersonal theory, and object relations theories, have pointed to the consistency with which such symptom constellations have been characterized as adaptive mechanisms for sustaining life (Fairbairn, 1952; Fromm-Reichmann, 1961; Winnicott, 1975).

Over the course of many sessions, there were increasing indications of the defensive aspects of Ms. A.'s psychotic symptoms and her intermittent confusion between inner and outer reality. At first, I had wondered if she experienced me as being neglectful and devouring, or as a representation of the helpless infant who needed protection from vehement hostility and destructiveness. Another of my initial concerns was that if intimacy signified annihilation, then what would be the outcome of emotional contact between us if my questions were felt to be attacks? In fact, we learned that Ms. A had not been completely free of the painful belief that I might invade her, engulf her and rob her of her identity, if she recovered more fully. Her disclosure of her memory earmarked death anxiety's unfolding in the transference. Consideration was given to her latent communication of the yearning for symbiotic merger and the failure of her psychotic defenses in the course of our interactions. Psychoanalytic clinicians, of all theoretical orientations, would listen for screen memories of early breakdown, family disturbance, and acts of cruelty, to which Ms. A might have been subjected.

In the single report of Ms. A.'s memory, she fashioned a lucid statement about her disordered thinking and her internal object relations in death imagery. By flights into psychotic withdrawal, she had historically protected herself not only from interpersonal dangers, but also from devouring internalized objects which dominated her psychic world. During her adolescence, Ms. A. seemed to have withdrawn in order to avoid the threat of death, and annihilation, and to have sought survival through symbiotic fusion. Her symbolic language demonstrated an initially ambiguous, ominous message about death anxiety and annihilation fears which steadily emerged in the transference. A misguided strategy of innate intelligence was contained in her retreat from sanity and her sustained array of symptoms. Despite their deficits in mental structure and ego functioning, the intelligence of such a characterological stance stamps schizophrenic patients' symptoms with the same symbolic fear of life and death endemic to the neurotic's death anxiety.

The exploration of Ms. A.'s memory, and its ties to the cataclysmic anxiety in her regressions, helped to clarify the nature of her childhood experience, and the influence of death anxiety on the exacerbations of her schizophrenic illness. The identification and working through of these issues, in the therapeutic interaction, hastened her reintegration and her increased sense of freedom from depression and primitive anxiety. In addition to Fairbairn, Little, and Winnicott, other psychoanalytic theorists have also noted that the resolution of death anxiety facilitates the development of a healthy transference object relationship (Rosenfeld, 1952; Searles, 1961; Spotnitz, 1969).

Death Anxiety and Schizoid States

From a contemporary psychoanalytic perspective, death anxiety, with its juxtaposition of the potential for life and death, lies close to the heart of the therapeutic inquiry. At points of potential change, self and object images of death anxiety fuel resistances as the work of analysis threatens security operations, and uncovers primitive disassociations. The transference remains the major arena for the working through of death anxiety and its gradual resolution via the unconscious upheavals of both neurotic, and more disturbed types of patients. As patients unconsciously seek to merge with the analyst, or to separate and individuate in harmony with the analytic movement, depression and ambivalence about death can lie close at hand. Object relations theorists, especially, have noted that, with schizoid patients, primitive anxieties remain powerful, and the fear of death emanates from a truly fragmented self. A. Freud, Klein and Little all stressed that, to the extent that self and object are perceived as identical, and fused in the transference, separation symbolically represents annihilation. Death anxiety is crystallized in transference states with either relatively healthy, or more seriously ill patients, as analysis facilitates characterological change and differentiation from internalized objects.

At stake, for both schizoid and borderline patients, is the psychodynamic linkage between separation anxiety, depression and intense annihilation anxiety, as the analytic process initiates resistances in the transference. As a result of preverbal terrors of fragmentation, disintegration, and loss of body integrity, disjunctive anxieties, and fears of the loss of the self are revitalized in analytic work. Following about a year of treatment, Mr. B., a student in his early twenties, who had many schizoid features, reported the following dream.

> I was both at home in my bed and at the office. I was paralyzed, tried to move, and couldn't, but my eyes were open. I thought a soul came into my room and tried to grab me and that I was falling into an abyss. I thought something terrible had happened at the office and it did - an explosion. I was outside it, but also inside it, and it all depended on me. The other guys escaped, but I didn't. It was like a magical universe. I could make the explosion just by thinking about it. I thought myself out of there and that I have to be careful

about what I think-All the things happen.   I was afraid everyone would die in the explosion.   When I was in bed, I thought, I'm really a warlock.   I can make anything happen. I'm better than they are.   I was a warlock because I could get away in my bed.   I could move, and I could move my fingers twice, so I knew that the explosion hadn't worked.

Even though this man possessed generally adequate judgement, and reality testing, in both dreams and waking life, he felt the need to resort to magical, dissociated states in which his powers were limitless, and one aspect of his identity was that of a warlock.   This identity fragment highlighted Mr. B.'s omnipotence, and the infantile fantasies which counteracted his more conscious feelings of shame and inferiority.   The dream's manifest content reflected his underlying rage, his controlling demandingness in intimate relationships, and his alienation from his feelings.   In the dream, the deadly explosion occurred in two places, and the word, office, had two possible meanings, namely, Mr. B.'s place of part-time employment and my office.   As the therapeutic investigation touched his grandiosity, his hidden feelings of superiority, and his fear of being influenced, he began to fear equally that I might overpower, and paralyze him, and that he might have to kill me.   Classical and Kleinian analysts might hear in this dream, the patient's hatred, envy and guilt displaced onto the soul, as well as references to primal scene fantasies. While interpersonal analysts might emphasize the current implications of Mr. B.'s childhood omnipotence, and his necrophilic tendencies, clinicians who have been most influenced by Fairbairn and Guntrip might conclude that the loss of his dissociated secret warlock self, and his evil powers, signified submission to an internalized persecutory object.

The therapeutic encounter took on the emotional quality of a life and death struggle which was experienced in the transference and the countertransference.   Mr. B.'s unconscious struggle to retain his use of detachment and splitting dictated a defensive counterassault on efforts to assist him towards self-knowledge and growth.   At stake was the disassociation of his infantile self in a magical world, of primitive terrors, where whims and needs could be satisfied by a mere expression or the slightest of gestures.   Close, intimate contact signified the loss of magical control, together with mutually destructive fusion and annihilation anxiety.   Our analysis of the explosion in the dream paralleled our attempts to learn the stimuli for Mr. B.'s fragmentation in the sessions, and the reawakening of his death anxiety. The dream symbolism expressed the collaboration of his internalized attachments with his characterological defenses in a novel blending of illusion and reality.

This patient's resistance to change amounted to more than a failure in the development of adequate internal psychic structure. His resistances denied the impact of the analysis. They defended him against the recognition of his sadism, his terror of being obliterated and his dread of falling into an abyss. They also unconsciously aimed to keep his infantile, warlock self alive. Beginning with Freud, a variety of psychoanalytic theorists have ascribed characterological trends, vividly conveyed in the transference-countertransference, to the enactment of the patient's primitive anxieties and object relations patterns.

Summary

Both Fromm and Fairbairn amended Freud's death instinct theory, just as they significantly altered personality theory and clinical practice. Fromm advocated heightening the tensions between the patient's life-affirming and life-destructive forces in order to bring about characterological change. Fairbairn worked interpretatively in his exposition of object ties which were present in both psychosexual and more infantile anxieties. Historically, transference has been understood as not only an expression of, but also as a solution to, unconscious needs and primitive anxieties. Some existentialist investigators, like Ernest Becker, went further than the psychoanalytic theorists by viewing transference as a kind of heroic struggle the person engages to assure immortality. The clinical work with the two patients mentioned, in this chapter, suggested a honeycomb of death and annihilation fears and archaic forms of relatedness in the transference. Death anxiety is surmountable when merger with the analyst gives way to healthy identifications, and transferential patterns recreate the patient's unique blend of character traits and world of inner objects. According to Freudian, object relations and interpersonal theories, the analytic uncovering of death anxiety contributes to the healing process of the therapeutic dialogue. The relinquishment of unhealthy character trends is facilitated by the resolution of both neurotic levels of death anxiety and more disorganizing annihilation anxieties.

As death imagery increasingly becomes the metaphor in analytic work for patients' internalized object relations, death anxiety may take the form of fusion with the good object, who will be a source of protection and nurturance, or with the persecutory object, who will attack. In spite of the existentialists' suppositions, transference cannot simply be defined as the universal childhood wish for protection from death. Fairbairn, Fromm-Reichmann, Guntrip, Sullivan, and Winnicott each explained with clarity and compassion the means by which security operations have kept disturbed patients psychologically alive. This relatively short survey of the concept of death anxiety in psychoanalytic theory has cataloged ways in which the psychoanalytic process reverberates with anxieties about life and death at each therapeutic interaction. The giving up of the patient's symptoms and character trends may signify further disruptions of self continuity or the loss of the self and the object. Each moment of growth, or resistance, potentially vitalizes unconscious annihilation fears, so-as-to complicate the specific psychodynamic and characterological pattern which is being addressed.

Freedom from depression and death anxiety grows out of the reorganization of the self in the analytic process. The analyst's presence, as significant other and transferential object, elicits the patient's characteristic mode of experiencing and defending against primitive anxieties. Summarizing his interpersonal theory of regressive tendencies in disturbed patients, Sullivan concluded that schizophrenia and schizoid phenomena took place when the self failed to exclude "primitive processes", or primitive anxieties, from awareness. In the next several chapters, I will explore resistance and countertransference aspects of clinical work with annihilation anxieties, and I will discuss how the emotionality of fusion undermines the reality of separation and the finality of death.

CHAPTER FIVE

Primitive Anxiety and Resistance

Anxiety and fear of real loneliness merge where they are an anticipation of the fear of the ultimate isolation and separation, of the inconceivable absolute loneliness which is death.

Frieda Fromm-Reichmann

Resistance and transference were designated by Freud (1914) as the starting points of every analytic procedure. In *The Problem of Anxiety*, Freud's (1926) expanded concept of anxiety established the groundwork for a widespread analysis of resistance and instinctual dangers. Although they were originally seen by Freud as manifestations of an antilibidinal force to be overcome in the patient, resistances are now viewed, in clinical practice, as communications about the patient's fears of both the analysis itself and psychological growth. Whether they are composed of brief evasions and lapses of attention, or willful refusals to reveal associations and missed sessions, resistances have been identified, in psychoanalytic theory, as a retreat from contact with the analyst, and a withdrawal from the anxiety inherent in the psychoanalytic process. In each of the three psychoanalytic clinical models, resistances have been closely tied to conceptions of anxiety, and to the role of the analyst in promoting psychological change. Resistances maintain character trends, and inevitably persist, because of unconscious defenses, as well as deficits within the self and the ego. Resistances likewise consist of concurrent intrapsychic and interpersonal events which demonstrate unconscious fears of intimacy and change. Just as they indicate anxiety about involvement in analysis, resistances simultaneously express unconscious annihilation anxieties and primitive fears of mourning which become an intrinsic part of transference patterns.

Introduction

The previous chapter examined the psychodynamic relationship between death anxiety, separation anxiety and depression, which is particularly manifest at points of resistance to psychic individuation and characterological change. This chapter will continue these themes by harnessing a discussion of primitive anxiety to the sources of resistance, and it will outline the overall functions of resistance, as they have been defined in the history of psychoanalytic theory. What the existentialists labelled, existential anxiety, and what Fromm-Reichmann referred to as the fear of "inconceivable loneliness", I have preferred to call death anxiety, in order to emphasize the depression and the fears of annihilation and mourning inherent in both neurotic, and more disturbed states of inner disorganization. According to the interpersonal and relational models, death anxiety and other primitive anxieties make their presence felt at moments of resistance to potential change, as the patient vacillates in psychic individuation and comes into conflict with the internal objects. Guntrip (1962) detailed such conflicts in states of existential anxiety, while Fromm (1964, 1973) highlighted the death fears in ill-advised, neurotic, existential choices. The terms, death anxiety and primitive anxiety, will again be used, here, to refer to not only the anxiety and depression in neurotic death fears or preoccupations, but also to the terror of annihilation which accompanies the anticipation of loss of the object and the individuated self. As a prelude to discussing the functions of resistance, this chapter will include a review of the role of separation fears in primitive anxiety, in addition to clinical material which will illustrate primitive anxiety's impact in resistance and countertransference anxiety.

According to Sullivan, Klein, Fairbairn, and Guntrip, the prospect of characterological change intensified the primitive anxieties and dissociated terrors of the inner world. As I have previously noted, primitive anxiety includes powerful, archaic anxieties which exceed simple conflict and threaten the eradication of the self, such as the simultaneous fear of death and the fear of psychotic disorganization. To the extent that the slow process of emotional growth remains equated with fears of death, identity loss, and object loss, ambivalence persists about the prospect of any substantial psychological change.

A docile, austere, colorless college student in his mid-twenties suffered from study inhibitions and numerous psychosomatic ailments. During a session the day after his last final examination of the semester, he reported having difficulty being self-reflective because of his lethargic mood and general fatigue. As he reviewed the events of the previous day, it became apparent that he made no mental connection between his feeling of tiredness and his having been out celebrating with his friends most of the previous night. His insensitivity to his body and his mind made explicit his circumscribed thought disorder in relation to time and causality. In the following session he remembered having woken up at age six or seven to find that his parents had secretly given him a short haircut while he had been asleep in bed. At that point, it seemed that his previous therapy had not fully explored the defensive aspects of his thinking impairment or the depths of his multiple anxieties concerning mental and physical integrity. This patient's dismemberment of his own reasoning ability insulated him against disintegrative fears of change.

Primitive anxieties may be experienced as either a surrender of the self and the body, or an annihilation of the self and the object in transference. As unintegrated, disassociated aspects of experience are relived with the analyst, primitive anxieties increasingly influence patterns of resistance and fears of change.

Wolstein (1986) observed that it was not until the 1930's that resistance analysis came into its own. At that time, A. Freud delineated the ego defense mechanisms, and Sullivan, Horney and Fromm had begun to postulate that interpersonal security operations were essential aspects of resistance. Resistance analysis currently proceeds on several levels of investigation of overlapping intrapsychic and interpersonal processes. First, resistances demonstrate the patient's defensive style for dealing with the anxiety of conflict and the anxiety of intimacy. Second, resistances illuminate the patient's internalized object relations, and their manifestations in the dissociated feelings which underlie character organization. In addition, resistances point to the significance of transference/countertransference exchanges which recreate the person's relational patterns and family dynamics. Resistances also serve as psychic guideposts to the progress of an analysis, and to the effects of the analyst's relatedness and contributions. Finally, resistances express the patient's terror of the unconscious meanings of growth and change. During any analytic session, growth, for the analyst, includes awareness of countertransference anxiety and countertransference resistance as obstacles to the patient's maturation. Growth, for the patient, implies the courage to use the process and the analyst's emphatic involvement in overcoming fears of change as well as flaws of character. Resistance analysis thus provides hypotheses about defensive movements towards or away from integration and growth.

Primitive Anxiety and Separation Anxiety

Death anxiety, in the neurotic, is inexorably tied to depression and to unconscious fears of losing the object and the self. For the psychotic, primitive fears of disintegration and annihilation have a more exaggerated basis. In contrast to the early Freudian reliance on castration anxiety, and the Kleinian emphasis on the death instinct, Fromm and Fairbairn accounted for death anxiety as a reflection of the helplessness of the poorly individuated self and a retreat from problematic internalized attachments. On the basis of their work, neurotic individuals, like the protagonists in many of Kafka's stories, can be characterized as fearing and wishing for a loss of the self at the brink of insight and positive emotional change. Anna Freud (1951) discussed the developmental course of such separation anxieties in neurotic children. She hypothesized that, when children equate separation with total abandonment and death, the feared loss of the parent will be even more frightening than children's anxieties about their own death. The physically healthy child, who experiences intense death anxiety, may struggle with anxiety about losing both the actual parent and the parent's inner representation. If the child retains the infantile perception of a lack of differentiation from the parents, then separations may be unconsciously perceived as annihilation. Conversely, for the depressed, suicidal child, death may be wished for as a merger and reunion with the lost good parent.

Severely phobic children, particularly school-phobic children, reveal these dynamics in their unconscious terror of separation from the parents, in which school attendance signifies either the parents' death or their own annihilation. Not attending school becomes the safest way of keeping both the parents and the child alive and united. Until latency, children's cognitive development assigns a concept of death as separation and abandonment, in which the fear of the mother's death may not be fully distinct from the child's own death. internalized attachments and characterological Family psychopathology maintains children's unconscious equation of separation and growth with primitive anxiety and death anxiety.

For the adolescent and the adult, anxieties about death and other forms of primitive anxiety, are closely linked as reflections of both the insufficiency of defensive operations and incomplete individuation. The tormented neurotic, like the depressed adolescent and the fanatical cult member, alternately fears death and wishes for it as a giving up of the self. Borderline and psychotic patients' primitive anxieties disclose their use of fragmentation and mental disorganization as defenses against both separation anxiety and the threat of annihilation (Fromm-Reichmann, 1959). The prospect of growth, during analysis, heightens individuation conflicts as it reawakens primitive anxieties. Remnants of early terror and annihilation anxieties keep the adolescent and the adult rooted in childhood attachments. The scope of these primitive anxieties includes, in addition to anxiety about death and object loss, the fear of identity loss, the fear of loss of bodily integrity, the fear of psychosis, and the fear of early traumatic preverbal experience. The fear of a complete break with reality, like the fear of disorganization, implies a sense of passive immersion in the internal world and a fear of loss of control over cognition and perception.

Primitive anxieties are more readily translated into specific symptoms in psychotic or borderline patients, when the dual fears of personal annihilation and the death of the internal objects precipitate decompensations at the onset of psychological individuation. The less disturbed person, who is preoccupied with death, shares some of dread of the borderline or psychotic patient's primitive fears. Winnicott (1974) explored this dynamic relationship between the fear of death and the fear of breakdown in a posthumously published paper. He suggested that the fear of a breakdown could be traced to actual breakdowns which did occur during childhood. Psychotic illness, in this model, constituted a defense against early agonies in which ego organization had been threatened and there had been a reversal of the maturation process. Over the last three decades many authors, (Arieti, Fromm-Reichmann, Giovacchini, Jacobson, Searles) have written extensively about the defensive role of disorganized mental states in warding off early affects which might overwhelm the ego.   For the borderline or psychotic individual, death anxiety blends with more primitive terrors of ego disintegration and loss, whereas for the neurotic, it signifies the separation fears and depression of the childhood self.   All forms of primitive anxiety escalate at points of resistance and potential personality change.   Primitive anxieties intensify as the analytic process uncovers what has been disassociated at the emergence of resistance in transference and countertransference.

Clinical Material

Primitive anxieties rise closer to consciousness, in resistance-transference-countertransference patterns, as patient/analyst interactions assume the configurations of the internalized object relations.   Moreover, the psychodynamic links between, depression, death fears, and separation anxiety seem more apparent when they contribute to resistance and to countertransference anxiety.   The analyst's task with resistance lies in the appreciation of the complexity of the patient's anxieties and the willingness to help translate these anxieties into specific threats which are stimulated by the analytic relationship.   At moments when the patient and analyst become closely connected in the transference-countertransference, the prospect of either merger or separation may reawaken death anxiety and primitive anxiety.   At this point, I will refer to two clinical examples of primitive anxiety.   The first vignette will provide an illustration of neurotic death anxiety.   In the second instance, Winnicott's analysis of one of his own dreams, will be used to portray a more disturbed degree of primitive anxiety in resistance and countertransference.

A successful, young woman in her early twenties, felt confused and couldn't concentrate at the beginning of a session.   She reported depression, and anger at my not having helped her overcome a fear of traveling.   As she related her anxiety about flying on a business trip, which would bring new responsibilities in a position of greater authority, she remembered a dream.   The dream began with her riding in an elevator, and feeling terrified that its crash would result in her death.   In the dream, the elevator stopped at a floor in a building which seemed to resemble the patient's previous place of employment.   Just after the patient got off the elevator, in the dream, it did fall, as one of the cables gave way, and she found herself in terror looking out over the open space. A large dog then suddenly appeared, and either jumped or fell into the elevator shaft. The dream ended as the patient was thinking about comforting the dying dog. Her associations connected the anxiety in the dream with her identification with her mother, and with her own anxiety about the upcoming flight. My associations led me to question what I might have done to spur her indignation, and to wonder whether the elevator represented either her mother's body, or the elevator in the building where my office was located.

This patient's anxieties about death and loss were interwoven with her image of herself as an independent adult, who could leave home and arrive at an autonomous, professional identity. If the analytic relationship was symbolized by the elevator and the dog, then the dream suggested that either she felt out of control and annihilated, or that her success might kill me. These anxieties were emblematic of her unrecognized fear, and anger, that I would not be able to survive without her, and that my not providing her emotional support would destroy her efforts to feel like a separate, selfsufficient adult. This patient's sense of self as a capable, productive adult evoked her self-destructive character traits. The dream also signified her fear of abandonment and need for protection from the death of the analyst. It clarified the meaning of her mistrust and fear of depending on me. As a sketch of her inner object attachments, and her connection with herself, the dream depicted the patient's neurotic struggle to escape from loss, self-annihilation and destructiveness. It was initially less anxiety provoking for this woman to maintain her confusion in the sessions, and to remain frightened of flying, than it was to face the implication of her feelings. During analysis, protection will be sought from any self discovery, which might bring close to consciousness neurotic anxieties, or more nearly psychotic anxieties, associated with anticipated loss and annihilation.

At first blush, the analysis of the dream was haunted with the possibility of a variety of structural and dynamic interpretations. The dream symbolism suggested Freud's (1920) concept of the death instinct as a destructive instinctual force which could be directed against the individual. Yet, this same clinical phenomena, could easily have been organized as an example of Fairbairn's (1943, 1952) idea that the death instinct represented sadistic relationships with bad internalized objects. As I have noted, Fairbairn included internalized aspects of actual relationships in his concept of schizoid or primitive anxiety. His view superseded Klein's (1932, 1946) belief that the death instinct, per se, explained death anxiety and that it accounted for the origin of all anxiety. Furthermore, this patient's confusion and her elaboration of her anxieties in the dream, exemplified Fromm's notion of the fear of the loss of the self, which was inherent in neurotic death anxiety. Her unconscious equation of growth and constructive change with death and abandonment also illustrated Sullivan's, Fromm-Reichmann's and Searles's interest in the motivational power of the need to avoid loneliness and isolation.

Winnicott's concept of primitive anxiety did not emphasize character organization, as much as it chronicled environmental failures and the effect of intrusions on the young child. He concluded that such anxiety about annihilation was a truly primitive anxiety. In Winnicott's influential paper, *Hate in the Countertransference*, he focused his scrupulously observant eye on primitive anxiety and its expression in both countertransference and transference resistance. Winnicott reported that his considerable countertransference anxiety resulted in numerous errors with patients, until he recovered by means of a "healing dream".

> The dream had two phases. In the first... I felt severe anxiety as I might lose a limb... This would be ordinary castration anxiety.
> In the next phase of the dream... I had no right side of my body at all. This was not a castration dream. It was a sense of not having that part of the body...
> The first part of the dream represented the ordinary anxieties that might develop in respect of unconscious fantasies of my neurotic patients... The second part of the dream, however, referred to my relation to the psychotic patient. The patient was requiring of me that I should have no relation to her body at all, not even an imaginative one... Any reference to her body produced paranoid anxieties, because to claim that she had a body was to persecute her... At the culmination of my difficulties on the evening before the dream I had become irritated and had said that what she was needing of me was little better than hair-splitting. This had a little disastrous effect and it took many weeks for the analysis to recover...My own anxiety was represented in the dream by the absence of the right side of my body... This right side of my body was the side related to this particular patient... This denial was producing in me this psychotic

type of anxiety, much less tolerable than ordinary castration anxiety (Winnicott, 1947).

This dream dramatically illustrated the countertransference expression of primitive anxiety as well as its emergence in resistance and transference. Both Winnicott's irritation and the patient's paranoid stance initially served as resistances which defended both of them against annihilation anxiety that impeded the analytic progress. From the perspective of Racker's (1968) view of countertransference, (which will be elaborated in the next chapter) Winnicott's countertransference anxiety would have reflected the patient's primitive bonds with her internalized objects.

The anxieties of Winnicott's patient, like those of the patient in the previous example, represented simultaneous, intrapsychic and interpersonal processes. Both of these patients' resistances constituted defensive responses to different degrees of primitive anxiety, which was evoked by and recreated in the analytic relationship. Falling to one's death, and losing half of one's body, suggested the anxieties of internal relationships which could only be reluctantly relinquished. In order to achieve emotional growth, patients must face such dissociated feelings, highly threatening mental states and other residue of early emotional experience. Many authors have shared the sentiment that the attainment of maturity and self-awareness takes place in spite of primitive anxiety.

In summary, resistances register primitive anxiety's influence, along with the isolation of change, and the possible shame and guilt which come to light with the negative therapeutic reaction. Primitive anxiety's influence on resistance and countertransference occurs whether it corresponds to neurotic constellations of death anxiety, or to more psychotic dissociations and regressed transference states. The preceding summary of prevailing defensive processes in resistance has been derived from the changing concepts of resistance in the different psychoanalytic theoretical models. Resistances inevitably make defensive statements about anxiety-laden internalized relationships and intrapsychic states which are expressed most overtly with the analyst in an interpersonal context.

Concepts of Resistance

Classical Freudian theory disseminated an intrapsychic view and drive theory concepts of resistance. Interpersonal and ego analytic definitions of resistance placed a greater emphasis on defenses and cultural aspects of anxiety and the self. The Freudian, interpersonal and object relations' notions of resistance have reflected contrasting approaches to the analyst's role, although all of the concepts of resistance evolved from Freud's identification of resistance with anxiety. Resistance assumed great importance in classical Freudian theory, especially with the concepts of transference resistance and transference neurosis. In interpersonal theory, resistance served as the counterpoint to the transference/countertransference harmonies of participant observation. Object relations theorists have generally made less extensive use of the concept of resistance. However, they have relied heavily on the concept of transference resistance in their exposition of character as the person's simultaneous efforts to remember and to forget infantile relational patterns. Racker, for example, described resistances as infantile processes which defended against the repressed, i.e. the transference. Attention may therefore be drawn to any resistance: first, as an expression of anxiety, second, as a manifestation of character and defenses, third, as an outgrowth of interpersonal processes and unconscious needs during analysis, and fourth, as an indication of both ego-function deficits and internalized object-relations. These concepts were devised by Freud, Reich, Anna Freud, Sullivan, Horney, Adler, Fromm, the ego psychologists and lastly the followers of Klein and the British school. Each concept corresponded to appropriate functions of the analyst in investigating and working with resistance as part of the therapeutic process.

Freudian Views of Resistance

Freud analyzed resistances according to their source, and their defensive nature according to the impulses which were being defended. Freud (1926) advocated understanding the nature of what was being repressed, by resistance, before proceeding with any other interpretation or clarification. Reich (1933), Fenichel (1939), and later Greenson (1967), integrated the contemporary Freudian technique of resistance analysis with the recommendations to the analyst to demonstrate that the patient is resisting, how and why the patient is resisting, and what it is that is being resisted. However, from the original classical Freudian perspective, analytic patients were said to resist in order to maintain repression, and the analyst's initial response to resistance was to ascertain its defensive properties and the id content which had been repressed.

Reich (1933) contributed an ego oriented definition of resistance as evidence of the patient's underlying neurotic character, along with his belief that transference resistance often remained a key impediment to the continuation of an analysis. Reich reasoned that neurotic character traits, as a whole, served as a defense in, what he called, the character resistances. From this point of view, the analyst first considered and analyzed character resistances and other latent resistances. The concept of resistance as a manifestation of particular defenses stemmed from Anna Freud's later enumeration of the mechanisms of defense and from her elaboration of specific defensive processes within the ego. These first concepts of resistance (those of Freud, Reich, Anna Freud, and the ego psychologists) derived from an originally intrapsychic conflict model in which resistances disclosed hidden character traits, latent anxieties, and unconscious defenses.

Interpersonal Views of Resistance

Sullivan (1954) offered no objection to the idea that anxiety was synonymous with resistance, since anxiety remained the chief obstacle to communication during therapy. Nevertheless, Sullivan (1953) held that anxiety first emerged during early development when the mother's disapproval led to lessened euphoria in the infant. For both the child and the adult, anxiety signified the anticipation of the loss of self-esteem and the sense of well-being. In interpersonal theory, the self system was the source of resistance to both therapeutic involvement and emotional growth. According to Sullivan's outlook, resistance and counterresistance were inseparable from the process of mutual influence in therapy, and consideration was given to the analyst's role in the creation of threats to the patient's security and self-esteem. Horney, Adler and Fromm contributed the concept of resistance as an expression of neurotic values and attitudes. Horney (1939) summarized the neoFreudian view of resistance with her observation that its source was the person's total interest in maintaining the *status quo*. For Horney, resistance referred to the energy with which thoughts and feelings were kept out of awareness in order to avoid recognition of unrealistic claims on life and illusions about oneself and others. From the humanistic/analytic perspective of Fromm, resistances perpetuated neurotic tendencies and values. The analyst's initial role was to note the specific context of the resistance and the threat of exposure of a neurotic character trend. The interpersonal analyst's awareness of (what Freudian and object relations analysts termed) ego-function and object-relations impairments concerned what the patient might be expressing by the presentation of a particular deficit in resistance. From the vantagepoint of the three psychoanalytic theoretical models, impairments in reality testing, impulse control and other ego functions were said to serve potentially defensive purposes throughout the course of any analysis.

Object Relations Views of Resistance

Klein (1946) and her followers related resistances in all types of patients, to splitting within the ego and to conflicts between dissociated parts of the ego. In object relations theories, resistances to growth were said to arise from the boundary impairments of self-object confusion, from the death instinct and also from the fear of primitive identifications. Kohut's clinical papers exercised his fluency as an interpreter of primitive anxiety from an object relations perspective. From Kohut's (1978) self psychology point of view, narcissism involved a partly nonspecific resistance to analysis, because of analysands' denial of unconscious wishes and dependency needs. For Kohut, the analyst's initial stance was to understand how specific resistances held back the activation of narcissistic needs, and the revelation of these needs in the narcissistic transference. This brief historical sketch of the different views of resistance in psychoanalytic theory mimics the variability of the different models' metapsychology.

Conclusion

There has been a common concern in both theory and practice with patients' defenses and the need to avoid the turmoil of inner differentiation and catastrophic anxieties. Whatever the function of a specific resistance in a particular session, attempts are routinely made to identify the wavering intensity of anxieties which accompany each movement of an analysis. All resistances manifest a personal style for maintaining hope, and ambivalence about psychic separation and growth.

Historically, analysts have linked anxiety to resistance and resistance to transference. Tying anxiety to resistance and transference-countertransference allows for scrutiny of primitive anxieties and their defensive elaboration in character organization.   The analysis of resistance delineates how the enactment of such patters brings to life, with the analyst, the legacy of family history and traumatic experience. Resistances thus comprise statements of confirmation of how analysis has evoked early profound anxieties, as well as more neurotic anxieties, which accompany the exposure of pathological traits and psychodynamic conflicts.   The interplay between depression, separation anxiety, and a disorganizing preoccupation with death and fragmentation comes close to describing the unconscious affects which include threats to the continuity of the self and the internal objects. The psychoanalytic process may be dreaded to the extent that   therapeutic engagement remains associated with annihilation and mourning.   Successful analysis allows for the use of the process in order to overcome primitive anxiety and to achieve emotional freedom.

CHAPTER SIX

Countertransference and Resistance

In brief, the analyst's depressive (and paranoid) anxiety is his emotional response to the patient's illness; and the patient's illness is itself a masochistic defense against the object's vindictive persecution.

Heinrich Racker

My interest in the interplay of countertransference and resistance has stemmed from my clinical work, and that of supervisees, with seriously disturbed patients. Even though they provide confirmation of the possibilities of health, resistances insinuate themselves into the mystery of defensive processes which unfold during both character consolidation and the therapeutic interaction. Countertransference reactions flourish with the graphic influence of anxiety on the patient's relatedness and the analyst's distinct emotional territory. In child and adolescent analytic work, the investigation of countertransference takes into consideration the unsparing effect of the patient's family interactions on the analyst's feelings and associations. This inclusive concept of countertransference extends Heimann's (1950) classic formulation of the need for the analysis of the totality of feelings which are evoked by the patient. Little (1951, 1957), Searles (1979, Winnicott (1947), Wolstein (1988) and other theorists have maintained interactive notions of countertransference in which the analyst's feelings mirror the patient's feelings. Racker (1968) echoed this view from a groundbreaking object relations orientation by stressing that the patient's feelings mirror the analyst's feelings in countertransference anxiety. Countertransference anxieties and countertransference resistances thus involve defensive responses not only to the patient, the transference and the patient's family, but also to the analyst's residual unconscious conflicts.

After a brief review of the concept of countertransference, my initial goal in this chapter will be to explore developmental and family influences on resistance and countertransference in child and adolescent treatment.   In the latter part of this chapter, I will expand one of my principal themes - primitive anxiety's impact in character trends - to include a discussion of countertransference anxiety.   I will offer the hypothesis that countertransference analysis with children and adolescents helps clarify the parents' role and that of the family process in the evolution of the youngster's character organization.   Countertransference patterns simultaneously reflect the adolescent's inner world and the product of his or her family dynamics.   As the analyst becomes both a transference figure and a real person in the adolescent's life, the underpinnings of characterological trends and family systems conflicts emerge in the resistance and countertransference.   This configuration of conflicts and attachments blends with the adolescent's defenses against reliving disorganizing anxieties in the analytic relationship.

Introduction

Freud (1910) first described countertransference as unrecognized emotional reactions which were induced by the transference, and he declared that resistances emanated from the ego (Freud, 1923). According to Freud's clinical theory, countertransference represented failures in neutrality and objectivity.   In all three psychoanalytic theoretical models, countertransference has referred to either emotional responses to the patient and the transference, or to personal elements which sway the analyst's feelings and responses.   Current models of the therapeutic efficacy of psychoanalysis adhere to an, essentially, interpersonal, object relational view in which resistance-transference-countertransference is seen as an ongoing interaction (Hirsch, 1987). In accordance with these models, it is my contention that, during child and adolescent treatment, parents' attitudes constitute a potential source of resistances which may emerge in the countertransference.   Parents' anxieties about treatment express the extent of their feeling threatened by the child's maturation and intimate involvement with the analyst.   As resistances elicit countertransference, and as countertransference gives rise to resistance, the patient's anxieties become evident, along with the analyst's anxiety and the family's contributions to the patient's psychopathology.   Analytic work with children and adolescents reawakens the analyst's anxieties and childhood feelings, as a result of the dual influence of the family process and the dialogue of the patient's inner objects. This idea- that resistance-transference-countertransference consists of an unconscious interaction which includes the child or adolescent, the analyst and the family- is in keeping with contemporary Freudian, interpersonal and object relations views of countertransference (Brenner, 1985; Epstein and Feiner, 1979; Racker, 1968; Sharpe, 1950).

Countertransference has been portrayed as a perceptual instrument which is sensitive to affective states which patients cannot verbalize (Heimann, 1950; Khan, 1979; Winnicott, 1947). Heimann and Racker elaborated subjective views of countertransference which implied the need for dealing with emotional responses induced by the patient, by the transference and by the analyst's emotional history. According to these dyadic conceptions of countertransference, countertransference responses clarify the patient's experience of the internalized object relations, and they delineate the impact of the family transactions on the analyst. Analysis of countertransference anxiety and countertransference resistance helps with the exploration of both the patient's involvement in the family system and the patterns of attachment with the internal objects.

Developmental Aspects of Resistance

Children's resistances were initially seen in psychoanalytic theory as reflections of their narcissism and limited anxiety tolerance. More recently, resistances have been characterized as a central, and, at times, hidden variable which accounts for much of a child's or adolescent's progress or negative therapeutic reaction (Marshall, 1972). Children's actions and facial expressions bristle with searing images of the unconscious conflicts which are inherent in their resistances. Adolescents' resistances similarly reveal crucial data about their character organization and their unconscious defenses. Resistances and defenses are swayed by developmental factors, to such an extent, that there are both generalized developmental sources of resistance and influences on resistance which are specific to particular developmental stages. Anna Freud (1947) highlighted this trend by observing the extent of children's defensive use of externalization and their consistent need for their parents as real figures. Cognitive abilities differ greatly among adolescents of the same age and similar type of character trends. Concentration ability, anxiety tolerance, and psychological mindedness all vary according to developmental levels. The variability in children's and adolescents' emotional and cognitive developmental growth rates is partly a product of the family process. Parental responsiveness provides the supportive ambience within which the child accomplishes maturation and the engagement of developmental tasks (Sullivan, 1953).

Adolescents' preference for action over thought and verbal expression and their limited tolerance for the anxiety of sexual conflicts represent two major developmentally based sources of resistance. Blos (1962) believed that:

> infantile conflicts are not removed at the close of adolescence, but they are rendered specific, they become ego syntonic-that is, they become integrated within the realm of the ego as life tasks.

According to Blos, adolescents' regressions to earlier psychosexual modalities engender much resistance and anxiety. A great many disturbed adolescents maintain little interest in becoming more introspective, and facing, in treatment, the insecurities of their sexual and aggressive conflicts. The ability to label feelings, and to distinguish thoughts from feelings and actions, varies with adolescents of the same age, as does abstraction ability and the capacity to use symbolic processes. Even though young children may be attentive to their own moods, and articulate about their inner experience, the ability to use language and symbolic processes to communicate psychological meaning is limited in many disturbed latency age children and adolescents. Along with great variability in short term and long term memory, adolescents may show flamboyant disregard for the concepts of time and causality. The anxious adolescent often finds that abstraction ability and problem solving skills become elusive during stressful moments. Logical thought and the reality sense come and go with the highly impaired adolescent child's affective turmoil. Adolescents regularly feel easily threatened by negative transference, and by negative feelings about their parents, because of their pressing need to maintain positive parental images in the face of both psychological individuation and separation from the family.

Early adolescence presents a plethora of opportunities for the influence of developmental factors on resistance and defenses. During early adolescence, heightened sexual strivings routinely stimulate anxiety, until the conflictual urges and fantasies are gradually integrated into self. Freud (1905) observed that young adolescents resent their parents and authority figures as part of the renunciation of the parents as Oedipal love objects. Anna Freud (1947) contended that the pubescent adolescent relies greatly on asceticism and intellectualization to counter the anxieties of puberty. Preadolescents' socially acceptable, repetitive "I don't know" statements and early adolescents' awkwardness with adults constitute additional developmentally based sources of resistance. For the adolescent, striking changes in psychological organization are accompanied by preoccupations with the body, and by daydreams, which serve stage specific defensive purposes. Adolescents' bouts of moodiness and self-conscious sensitivity are typical concomitants. Self-revelation and openness in the analytic relationship may remain quite threatening for adolescents, if self-awareness heightens conflicts about sexuality or any aspect of individuation. "I don't know" statements may also suggest that the young adolescent is afraid to develop ideas and opinions in the family, or that he or she wishes to be nurtured and taken care of in the transference. Adolescents universally lend their defenses and resistances to countering the anxieties of identity and ego reorganization.

Adolescents' feelings of defiance and rebelliousness, at times, convert talking into an unwelcomed submission of the self, and assign to the analytic relationship, the meaning of merger and fusion with analyst. Talking about body experience and sexuality can bring potentially more anxiety and shame than with adult patients. Fears of revealing negative material about families (and the fear of the loss of parental love) frequently remain covert developmental sources of resistance. Feelings of disloyalty and fears of abandonment will accompany positive emotional changes for the adolescent, if closeness with the analyst is perceived as an unsanctioned separation from the parents. Adolescent patients will become anxious and depressed at the prospect of both therapeutic involvement and emotional change, if their parents withdraw, as a result of equating growth and change with the renunciation of family ideology. Under these circumstances, adolescents' therapeutic alliances mask their unwillingness or inability to trust sufficiently to risk unfettered self-disclosure. Adolescents' lability and contradictory states of relatedness were sharply delineated in A. Freud's (1936) depiction of their affectivity.

They form the most passionate love relations, only to break them off as abruptly as they began them. On the one hand they throw themselves enthusiastically into the life of the community and, on the other, they have on overpowering longing for solitude. They oscillate between blind submission to some self-chosen leader and defiant rebellion against any and wary authority. They are selfish and materially minded and at the same time full of lofty idealism. They are esthetic but will suddenly plunge into instinctual indulgence of the most primitive character. At time their behavior to other people is rough and inconsiderate, yet they themselves are extremely touchy. Their moods veer between light hearted optimism and the blackest pessimism. Sometimes they will work with indefatigable enthusiasm and, a later time, they are sluggish and apathetic.

These same developmental factors, which make adolescents anxious about change, contribute to their hypersensitivity and ambivalence about the intimacy of the therapeutic relationship.   As transference and countertransference reactions stimulate resistances, the adolescent makes defensive use of developmental factors in struggling with both intrapsychic and family aspects of change.

Family Aspects Of Resistance And Countertransference

Parents' neurotic needs and family imbalances contribute to the adolescent's initial resistance to therapeutic involvement, just as they later influence resistances to emotional growth. When resistances are assessed from the point of view of countertransference, one can designate not only the family's role in the child's psychopathology, but also the emotional functions of the patient's developmental immaturities for the family. Current family systems theory's elaboration of Sullivan's interpersonal theory has accounted for the child's sacrifice of developmental opportunities in order to maintain family equilibrium. M. Klein (1948) and Friedman (1985) both emphasized that children feel unconscious guilt at the perception of having harmed their parents and at the perception of being responsible for their parent's emotional suffering.

Parents of children and adolescents, who are in analytic treatment, unconsciously induce guilt, while maintaining ambivalent feelings about the child's progress and involvement with the analyst. The maturing, autonomous child serves less well the emotionally damaged parent who uses the child to lower anxiety and to restore psychic balance. Parents fear the possible loss of their use of the adolescent child as either an aspect of the self or as a replacement for lost narcissistic supplies. They likewise fear the exposure of their own pathological relatedness as their character disturbance shapes family life in the present. In disturbed families, the parents' intense need for the child to maintain their psychopathology strongly conflicts with the youngster's emotional needs and strivings to separate from the parents.

> One such family demonstrated parental approval of a young adolescent's destructiveness, during an initial consultation, when the father smiled with impunity while telling me of his son's suspension from junior high school for very extensive vandalism of school property. The father's overt encouragement of his son's behavior was openly manifest in his smile which signified pride at his son's reenactment of his violent, aggressive impulses. The malevolent smile also signaled the father's unconscious derision of the prospect of treatment, along with his contemptuous dismissal of his son, as anything more than his symbiotic agent.

In such families, parents ignore and distort unhealthy character trends and assign neurotic meanings to the child's developmental needs and attempted mastery of developmental tasks.

In healthier families, parents resist children and adolescents' emotional involvement in analytic psychotherapy because of unacknowledged feelings of inadequacy and competitiveness, and because of their lapses in individuation with respect to their own parents. Children's positive transference reactions may lead to feelings of inadequacy or Oedipal rivalry in their parents, if the analyst is considered a better parent or a rival. Children's negative transference elicits confirmation of their parents' negative transference to the analyst. Parents' defensive organization, both as a couple, and as individuals, is therefore challenged by the child's or adolescent's commitment to analysis or analytic psychotherapy.

The reality of the child's sessions, together with the eventual emotional and behavioral changes, threatens parents' self- perceptions and self-delusions, by disrupting their use of projection, idealization, and splitting. Parents typically project and displace, onto children, feelings about themselves, their spouses, and their own parents, as they struggle with internalized object relationships and pathological identifications. Some parents feel envy, rejection, and rage as their child or adolescent successfully accomplishes developmental tasks which signify appropriate individuation. Disturbed parents' heightened anxiety may contribute to ego regression, or at least to the loss of an idealization of themselves, their spouses, and their own parents. As the adolescent patient matures, he or she becomes less willing either to behave, or to feel like disowned projections of pathological aspects of his or her parents. The adolescent becomes less likely to act out, in order to demand parental attention and love, or to express anxiety and wishes to retaliate. As a result of changes in parent-child interactions which result from the child's analytic treatment, disturbed parents become less defended against repressed feelings and transference states. It is profoundly disturbing for parents to experience depression, anger and paranoia which is stimulated by the experience of having their adolescents' treatment unravel their own defensive operations. Such parents may feel continually inadequate and insecure, in the face of the adolescent's emotional growth and the analyst's skill.

Clinical Material

A case vignette will advance the idea that resistance-transference-countertransference exchanges elucidate the impact of family processes on the child's or adolescent's developing self and character. Aspects of the following clinical example will stress the relevance of both intrapsychic and family factors in a specific interaction which occurred with a male adolescent patient. The analysis of my countertransference and hidden countertransference anxiety helped to clarify the dynamic sources of this boy's withdrawal and avoidance of age appropriate interests and relationships.

Robert was a bright, depressed, thirteen year old boy who had few friends and was a chronic underachiever at school. He lived with his divorced mother and three siblings, but he had no contact with his father, who had deserted the family when he was five years old. At the beginning of one session,

Robert described in minute detail the activities of his pet
snake, as he did repeatedly in most sessions, while saying very
little about himself. Consistent talk about reptiles seemed, for
him, a way of avoiding awareness of his loneliness, and the
humiliation of his failures and rejections at school. His
preoccupation with the pet, which he could control, kept at
bay the feeling of his mother's disappointment in him, and his
own disappointment about his lack of social and academic
achievements. As this patient again described his pet snake,
I stifled a yawn and the following interaction occurred:

Patient: Are you bored?

Analyst: What made you think I was bored?   Was it
           because I yawned?

Patient: You are bored.

Analyst: Was there something else in your mind just now?
          Were you wondering why I yawned like I was bored?

Patient: Everybody is always bored with me. My family
          yells at me that all I think about is snakes. I am
          boring. Snakes are the only thing I'm interested in.
          I can't help it.   It's not my fault.

Analyst: Did it seem like it was your fault when your
          father left?

Patient: Well, I used to think it was. He was always yelling
          at me, but I don't care now.

My brief feeling of boredom in the session gave way to curiosity
about what Robert was telling me about himself and his family. It
became clear that this boy felt unacceptable when he perceived that his
transferential father had lost interest in him. My momentary withdrawal,
and   recreation   of   the   family's   disapproval,   obscured   a
countertransferential emptiness and anxiety which seemed to echo
Robert's mental state. His obsessional reports about snakes evoked in me
a deadening detachment and withdrawal, which had arisen, in him, as
defenses against his feelings of worthlessness and abandonment. His
family's disapproval had contributed to his retreat into a world of barren
absence, and to further constriction of his interests and emotional life.
Robert's preoccupation with snakes suggested symbolic self images which
conveyed repulsiveness and unattractiveness combined with the wish for

potency. His feelings of shame and isolation detracted from his minimal efforts to establish relationships with peers, and they intensified his despair of gaining attention and nurturance, either at home, or in the transference. The grim degree of distance, which he maintained in the sessions, suggested the extent of his emerging obsessional, schizoid detachment from his emotional life. The initial boredom I felt had threatened to uproot my connection with Robert. My countertransferential withdrawal seemed to have been buoyed by his feeling of fragmentation and his sense of responsibility for his father's abandonment, as well as for the rejections by his peers at home and at school.

Robert evidenced little insight into his withdrawal, and only meager awareness of how he provoked the slights and rejections which added to his lack of curiosity and social interests. His depressive feelings arose, not only in the transference, but also in myriad daily interactions with his classmates and his family. These anxiety ridden states rendered him unable to deal with the underlying expression of grief, humiliation, and anger which often characterized his moods. His feelings indicated a depressive posture, within a family system of interactions, which was perpetuated by the failure to completely reintegrate after the loss of the father. As a result of Robert's dominant character trends and his internalization of the family dynamics and his parents' indifference, he had partially relinquished the developmental tasks of a thirteen year old. This vignette combined an analysis of dynamic family influences on evolving character trends, with a use of countertransference in which there was a participation with the patient's resistance (Cooper, 1987; Wolstein, 1975).

Countertransference Anxiety - Countertransference Resistance

Even if countertransference feelings convey elements of the analyst's unresolved conflicts, they contain responses to patients' most powerful anxieties. In forming the hypothesis that countertransference reactions illuminate the role of anxiety and family interactions in the adolescent's character organization, I have not made a hard and fast distinction between countertransference responses, which are stimulated by the patient, and those which stem from the analyst's emotional issues. Whether their source is the analyst's residual conflicts, the transference, or the family, countertransference anxieties direct attention to painful aspects of the patient's anxieties and internalized relationships. As the adolescent patient tries to elicit his or her family relationships in the analyst, countertransference anxieties reverberate with the patient's most primitive anxieties and transference states.

Countertransference anxiety records involvement with the patient's defensive efforts to avoid both neurotic and more primitive anxiety.

> A clear example of straightforward countertransference anxiety took place in one of my early sessions with a shy, depressed, very bright, sixteen year old girl who usually veered away from anxiety provoking subjects in spite of her considerable ability to be self-reflective. This girl generally stimulated feelings of warmth and concern in me, as though she were my daughter. As she described disagreements with her maternal grandparents, with whom she lived, I suddenly realized my discomfort and reluctance to refer to her alcoholic, abusive parents who had raised her until she was six. After some delibration, I mentioned my reluctance to the patient, and she started to cry. She slowly began to reveal her fear of her own disturbance and her fear of her identification with her parents' pathology and their violent outbursts. She had routinely relied on a massive use of denial and repression in order to insulate herself from these traumatic memories. Particularly persuasive among my initial countertransference reactions had been the prevailing force of denial. My avoidance and denial of the scope of the patient's anxieties had arisen from the shadows of her emotional history.

In contrast to my commonplace level of countertransference distress with this patient, a male therapist brought to supervision his anxiety filled work with a fifteen year old boy who brought him to the verge of tears of helplessness and frustration.

> The patient, who had many borderline features, verbally attacked the therapist and denigrated his competence, intelligence and integrity. This patient viciously insulted the therapist while devaluing all of his questions and interventions,

as well as his silence. As this boy's disruptive behavior escalated at school, he bragged during the sessions about his fantasies of blowing up his school with a bomb. This patient was so poorly differentiated from his paranoid, infantilizing parents that his ego impoverishment and grandiose posturing included homicidal fantasies which expressed his parents' hateful provocativeness.

The therapist's overwhelming anxiety and sense of inner fragmentation reflected a defensive response to the patient's use of splitting, his projective identification and his anticipation of mutual annihilation. Countertransference resistances imply unwillingness on the part of the analyst to identify personal sources of anxiety in countertransference feelings. Countertransference resistances are also implicit in the unwillingness to connect countertransference with the patient's intrapsychic fantasies and family transactions. Before exploring a number of such attitudes, which illustrate countertransference resistance, I will mention another clinical vignette which was evocative of possible countertransference anxiety.

Giovacchini (1985), who has written a great deal about countertransference anxiety, discussed the course of his office treatment of a very bright nineteen year old college student who made excellent progress after a period of hospitalization for schizophrenia. This patient used splitting and he maintained a defensive posture in the sessions by routinely having nothing to say. His disconnection, from both himself and his analyst, was expressed by a dream in which the patient and the analyst were in a dark room. The patient could not see the analyst in the dream and did not know whether Dr. Giovacchini was there in the room. The dream was interpreted in terms of the patient's psychic discontinuity and the lack of connection between his inner personality and the external object. However, the dream's literal manifest content was simply that the patient, and presumably, the analyst, could not see.

The elements of the dream suggested interpersonal and object relational questions about the potentially primitive anxiety inherent in the experience of feeling ignored and invisible. The analysis might have considered what the dream said about the status of the patient's individuation and his internalized relationships. What was symbolized by being ignored, by not seeing and by not being seen? Were there painful, traumatic aspects of either the family history, or the patient's early development which he had been forced to dissociate? Was this a family, with secrets, which needed to be kept hidden from the patient's conscious awareness?   What was it that the analyst didn't see, about the transference-countertransference contributions to the patient's detachment, and lack of having anything to say? What was it that the patient didn't want to see about the analyst or the analyst's feelings? A careful investigation of the latent countertransference anxiety might have clarified those defensive processes which were symbolized by the patient's (and the analyst's) failure to turn the light on in the room in the dream. From Winnicott's and Fairbairn's perspectives, the analyst's latent anxiety about the patient's not being seen, or acknowledged, might have been related to the source of the patient's madness, his need to entice and his retreat from inner objects. Khan (1974) likewise stipulated that silence could serve as a medium for the acting out of pathogenic infantile object relationships. The dream was interpreted along the lines of the patient's structural deficits. Yet, the countertransference anxiety and the primitive anxiety, which it might have registered, could have had very far-reaching implications.

Schowalther (1985) argued that there was usually some element of true countertransference in response to child and adolescent patients. He designated, as true countertransference, those reactions to a patient which are partially defensive and based on unconscious needs. In contrast to countertransference, counteractions were described as reactions, which were induced mostly by the patient, which would be induced by the same patient in other therapists. Marshall (1979) listed a number of frequent sources of countertransference resistance with children and adolescents, such as: the need to be liked or to gratify the child, the need to be preoccupied with change and the need to not feel sexual or aggressive feelings with children.   Identification with a child, or an adolescent patient as simply deprived, or as the victim of the family milieu, may obfuscate the depth of his or her character problems and disorganizing anxieties. I have increasingly come to believe that the unabashed need for protection from countertransference anxiety, as a response to the adolescent's most disturbing anxieties, entails an equally important source of countertransference resistance.

The wish to feel like a good parent in order to nurture the child or adolescent patient presents the possibility of countertransference resistance, as does the therapeutic stance that the adolescent is simply assisted with the completion of developmental stages. The refusal to meet with, or in any way involve, parents of adolescents in treatment may suggest the denial of countertransference reactions to the parents, or the denial of competitiveness and avoidance of their insecurity and jealousy. If the analyst is a parent, then countertransferential feelings may be threatening as displacements of feelings about one's own offspring. Clinicians' reluctance to hear signs of either a paternal transference, or a maternal transference implies the possibility of countertransference resistance. Parents' persistent ambivalence about adolescents' emotional progress in treatment has been stressed as another influence upon countertransference resistance. If adolescent therapists work in a setting where there is pressure for ironclad documentation of change from the parents or from the institution, then the suspension of interest in change in the therapeutic moment brings the prospect of disapproval as an additional source of countertransference resistance.

Countertransference resistances with adolescents evolve as an opaque pattern of avoidance of the patient's anxiety, the analyst's anxiety and the parents' anxiety, which occurs when the therapeutic interaction triggers defenses against acknowledging and dealing with the analyst's anxieties and affect laden memories. The specific avoidance entails either a lack of recognition of disassociated countertransference feelings, or a minimization of the influence of both anxiety and family processes on the analyst, and on the adolescent's impact during the sessions. In Racker's (1968) view, it was the analyst's identification with the patient's internalized objects which freed the analyst's archaic anxieties. As I mentioned in previous chapters, psychoanalytic theorists of each orientation have described archaic anxieties as primitive in order to emphasize their disorganizing and preverbal, aspects. Racker made this point in relation to the intensity of countertransference reactions with adult patients, which he explained, on the basis of the analyst's pathological defenses against unresolved conflicts and early anxieties. Racker's observations seem equally true of countertransference anxiety with adolescents. They seem more val'd than either the suggestion that children's provocativeness and closeness to unconscious processes overwhelms the analyst (Bornstein, 1948), or the idea that children and adolescents have a special ability to arouse unconscious impulses. It has been my impression that countertransference anxieties take on aspects of the patient, aspects of the parents and aspects of their interaction. Countertransference feelings constitute the analyst's unique personal response to the adolescent and the family, as well as to the adolescent's resistance and transference states.

Conclusion

I have drawn attention to a number of general points about resistance, as well as to countertransference anxiety, with adolescent patients. First, resistances are comprised of family, developmental, and dynamic components, since they are composed of both intrapsychic and interpersonal aspects. Second, countertransference illuminates the nature of the adolescent patient's intrapsychic reality, as well as the nature of his or her family experience. Third, the continuous family process, which is relentlessly manifest in resistance, remains a key intervening variable in the adolescent's maturational lags and unfolding character traits. Finally, the analysis of countertransference and countertransference anxiety pinpoints the adolescent patient's core anxieties and their relationship to character development.

Countertransference feelings make apparent the analyst's responsiveness to the patient and patient's internalized object relations. If the analyst is not resisting, then the content of countertransference follows the course of empathic identifications with the patient and the path of reactions to the patient's deepest anxieties. Sensitivity to countertransference anxiety brings into focus the threats to the adolescent's self continuity. Countertransference anxieties confirm how the patient's defenses, and resistances aid in repudiating the myth of the "impersonal analyst" (Little, 1951). Countertransference anxiety is implied, when there are reaction formations, denials of feeling, or an overidentification with either the patient or the parents. For example, countertransferential reaction formation is paramount, when the analyst's wish to rescue a young patient from suffering during a session, obscures the wish to cling to the patient in an unconscious identification with the parents' overinvolvement. Many authors have made these points with respect to adult patients, since countertransference anxiety has been portrayed as the crucial signpost to the analysand's character and inner world. These issues have been thoroughly examined by Fairbairn (1952), Giovacchini (1989), Searles (1979) and many other theorists. In response to a question he asked Fairbairn about countertransference, Guntrip (1969) quoted Fairbairn as saying:

> You may do more harm to a patient if you are afraid of countertransference.

In similar spirit, Racker (1968) observed that analysts' denial and rejection of countertransference amounted to:

> unresolved struggles with their own primitive anxiety and guilt.

In conclusion, countertransference brings to light the influence of anxiety and family processes on the patient's maturation and character development. The therapeutic engagement with adolescent patients potentially threatens parents' defensive operations, both as couples, and as individuals. Family influences on resistance and countertransference therefore need to be subjected to analytic scrutiny. Countertransference anxieties afford the opportunity to explore the meaning of resistances, and to locate with precision the experienced threats of disorganization and internal differentiation. With adolescents, the twofold therapeutic task consists of defining and counteracting the family's negative impact on the developmental process, in addition to addressing the adolescent's contribution to his or her own pathological character traits. Countertransference anxiety confirms the dynamic and family implications of the analyst's participation with the patient. Developmental, dynamic, and family-interpersonal factors all merit analysis as part of the interpersonal matrix. Resistance-transference-countertransference exchanges clarify the adolescent's efforts to move towards health while emerging from the family and the internal object world. Countertransference resistances hint at a lack of openness in the assessment of how analytic treatment has evoked the patient's anxiety, the parents' anxiety and the analyst's potentially primitive anxiety.

PART III

ADOLESCENTS' CHARACTER PATHOLOGY

CHAPTER SEVEN

BORDERLINE ADOLESCENTS

The child...who is chiefly concerned with the innate problems of personality integration and with the initiation of a relationship with environment is not yet at the depressive position in personal development.

Donald Winnicott

...One awakens from some utterly unknown events in practically primordial terror, in this stage, one is on the border of complete disintegration of personality...

Harry Stack Sullivan

Borderline adolescents' interactions express regressed, labile forms of relatedness. Primitive anxiety disrupts their relatedness in ways which signal not only the failure of defensive operations, but also impairments in the maturational process. Borderline adolescents' transference reactions present defensive elements of omnipotent grandiosity and paranoia which derive from their lack of ego integration. The intermittently symbiotic quality of such transference responses concertizes the extent of their psychopathology.

In this chapter, I will summarize the principal clinical features and the major psychoanalytic studies of borderline adolescents' character formation. As part of this summary, my primary aim will be to describe how omnipotent symbiosis and paranoia characterize borderline adolescents' transference reliving of their disturbed object relationships. In tracing borderline adolescents' clinical features, I hope to illuminate the jarring effects of their annihilation anxiety, as well as their relative lack of differentiation from internalized objects. A secondary objective will be to use clinical material in order to elaborate Freudian, interpersonal and object relations views of borderline adolescents' character features. The brief clinical examples I have chosen will demonstrate that undifferentiated states of primitive anxiety about annihilation of the self and the object are frequent aspects of borderline adolescents' subjective experience. Enormous clinical benefit can be derived from allowing borderline adolescents' regressed transference reactions to develop, and analyzing the nuances of mutual interaction which stimulate their unfolding.

Introduction

A very brief case vignette will illustrate these patients' fluid sense of identity, their symbiotic transference attachments and their failure to elude primitive anxiety. The use of the term, symbiotic transference, refers to psychic fusion in which there is a lack of differentiation and psychological boundaries, and not simply to processes of identification with the analyst or internalization of aspects of the analyst.

Sarah, a fifteen year old adolescent girl with borderline traits, routinely complimented her female therapist about the therapist's hairstyle. At one point, when Sarah was touching her own hair, she said to her therapist: "I like your hair. Long hair is pretty. It's cut well". Later, she asked in reference to another girl, whom she knew, "Are you going to see her hair too?" The former statement was made with an intonation which suggested that Sarah was inside her therapist's body. The latter question was asked with a tone of voice which indicated that the second girl's hair was not part of her body. Hovering in a haze of confusion, Sarah's thought processes revealed a curtailed sense of identity and a dread of physical disintegration. Sarah's preoccupation with hair reflected her vacillating body image and her loss of the mental representation of the therapist. Her self experience was apparently one of being hair on her therapist's head. Both her friend and her therapist seemingly existed for Sarah as either disembodied bits of hair, or as hair on her own head. In instances such as the above interchange, she fused with her therapist in response to an undifferentiated, nearly psychotic anxiety.

The three psychoanalytic models of metapsychology would reconcile aspects of this kind of clinical situation on the basis of divergent explanations. The ego psychology Freudian model would hold that the boundary between self and other became blurred resulting in an interchange of self and object representations. Sullivan's observations about the terrible suffering and isolation of adolescents, who were subject to schizophrenic episodes, included one of the first accounts of the disorganizing quality of such adolescents' primitive anxiety. Writing around the same time period, Fairbairn (1943) claimed that a great many psychotic breakdowns during adolescence represented transient manifestations of intense schizoid or primitive anxiety. In keeping with Winnicott's (1951) concept of transitional relatedness, object relations theorists have suggested that borderline adolescents lose the visual representation of the internal object and fail in attaining adequate ego differentiation and full recognition of the body self. In fact, Sarah's merger with her therapist seemed to include a shared body image, prior to a stage of greater ego differentiation. The treatment sessions were replete with examples of interactions which conveyed this patient's boundary confusion and fragmentation. Although this patient experienced herself and others largely as merged fragments, borderline adolescent patients typically display a number of related ego deficits and intense annihilation anxiety.

Primitive Anxiety and Ego Deficits

For borderline children and adolescents, disorganizing, primitive anxieties remain dominant. Their deficits in ego functioning are compounded by psychic states, which were described by Sullivan, Klein, Fairbairn and Winnicott, in which either fusion or separation from the internal object feels like death or annihilation. Borderline adolescents both fear and seek symbiotic fusion in its many manifestations. Their ego integrity continues to be easily compromised, and their patterns of relatedness are tinged with omnipotence and paranoia. Socially inappropriate or bizarre behavior on their part embodies defensive attempts to avoid death or annihilation anxiety. Borderline adolescents' symptomatic behavior also represents, both enactments of primitive anxiety, and unconscious attempts to recreate early internal object relationships involving the threat of annihilation. As a synthesis of the psychoanalytic writings on borderline adolescents, I will review clinical studies of these patients' impaired relatedness and deficiencies in ego functioning. Most of the psychoanalytic theorists, who have studied borderline adolescents, have espoused a developmental arrest model of the etiology of borderline personality disorders. All of the theorists I will mention have taken into account the broad range of borderline adolescents' symptomatic behavior. Only a few authors have stressed borderline adolescents' primitive anxiety as a core element of their psychopathology.

Both theorists and researchers, alike, have noted the primacy of borderline patients' shifting levels of ego functioning. In Freudian theory, borderline adolescents' deficits have seen said to result from a failure of signal anxiety, a lack of object constancy, and a failure of the ego's synthetic function. A detailed analysis of Kernberg's and Kohut's positions on the etiology of borderline disorders falls beyond the scope of this chapter. However, Kernberg's (1975) overview of borderline personality organization emphasized that the diagnosis of the borderline disorder was dependent on characteristic ego impairments. Chronic diffuse anxiety was a key symptomatic feature of these patients. Kernberg classified such severe lack of anxiety tolerance as the borderline patient's non-specific ego weakness. Bemporad's (1982) follow-up studies of borderline children and adolescents have found extensive character disturbance during these patients' early adulthood. As adults, these individuals have exhibited extremely poor adaptive functioning. As children and adolescents, their chief diagnostic features included inappropriate attachments and intense anxiety which approached panic states and fears of annihilation. In terms which were similar to those I am using, Bemporad maintained that the fears of borderline children and adolescents are rooted in anxiety about mutilation, self-destruction and the end of the world. Borderline adolescents' primitive anxieties are thus more closely akin to those of psychotic patients. Little's (1990) account of her analyses contained a number of examples of the dehumanizing terror of her own primitive anxiety which she relived during her treatment. Her personal descriptions of overwhelming anxiety about annihilation, dismemberment and abandonment provided insight into the experience of individuals who are developing borderline and psychotic disturbance. In an earlier report of her treatment cases, Little (1965) found that primitive anxiety states were common in her adult borderline patients.

Eckstein and Wallerstein (1957) noted that borderline youths' tenuous ego organization was the basis for their fluctuation between neurotic and psychotic states. Giovacchini (1963) suggested that borderline patients' deficient object relations stem from a lack of functional introjects, that is, memories of early nurturant experience which help expand the ego's executive functions. Kernberg, Masterson and Rinsley all elaborated etiologic models of borderline adolescents which highlighted these patients' failures in, what Mahler (1968) called, the reapproachment crisis of ego and object relations development. Kernberg (1975, 1979) pointed to the centrality of several specific deficits which underlie the symptoms of borderline adolescents and adults. As I have noted, these deficits included the emergence of primary process thinking, and non-specific ego weakness. According to Kernberg's theory, early defenses, such as denial or splitting and the impaired integration of self and object representations were major deficits. He attributed borderline adolescents' pervasive difficulties with aggression to their prevalent use of splitting and projective identification. Pine's (1974) studies of borderline children have added several important considerations, in particular, that no one symptom can be considered pathopneumonic of borderline psychopathology.

Paulina Kernberg (1979, 1982) observed that, for borderline children, a cluster of specific symptoms does not accurately represent their clinical status. She believed that the criteria for the diagnosis of borderline personality disorder in a child should take four factors into consideration. These deficits involved shifting levels of functioning, a poor identity sense, the inability to feel pleasure and the inability to accept responsibility for behavior. Masterson and Rinsley (1975) closely based their work with borderline adolescents on Mahler's (1971, 1975) theoretical constructs. They each attributed the borderline personality disorder in childhood and adolescence to early childhood failures in separation-individuation. Both Rinsley (1978, 1980) and Masterson (1972, 1974) depicted the mothers of borderline youths as rewarding regressive behavior and discouraging healthy autonomous functioning. According to Masterson's view of, what he labelled, the split-object relations unit, the adolescent borderline condition arises from dual sources. The impetus for separation-individuation in the child leads to a withdrawal of maternal supplies. Regression is thus rewarded. The push for individuation simultaneously gives rise to an abandonment depression and a narcissistic orally fixated ego. In spite of the clinical value of these theories of borderline ego impairment, a number of authors, such as P. Kernberg, have cautioned against a purely developmental, psychological explanation for the etiology of borderline character trends without any mention of the role of organic brain dysfunction. Organic impairments which interfere with the child's attention and memory certainly have considerable impact on mental images and object constancy. Another note of caution has been sounded by researchers who have compared the object relations of borderline adolescents with borderline adults' object relations patterns. There has been only limited empirical support for the assumption, which is implicit in Mahler's and Kernberg's theories, that the continuum of adolescent and adult psychopathology directly corresponds to the continuum of early development (Westen, 1990).

Clinical Features

Adolescents diagnosed as having a borderline syndrome present varying symptoms and interpersonal problems. They are characterized by variations not in only in the stability of behavioral control, but also in the integration of thought and affect, and the potential for regression into brief psychotic states. A body of published knowledge has emerged, largely in the Freudian and object relations literature, which has emphasized the impact of the very mother-child bond on the development of the borderline adolescent's object relationships and ego functioning (Eckstein and Wallerstein 1954, 1957; Fintzy, 1971; Giovacchini, 1972; Mahler, 1968, 1971, 1975). Their defenses seem to remain developmentally immature, and their lack of effectiveness in warding off intense anxiety contributes to their symptom formation. As I have mentioned, borderline patients' destructive and self-destructive actions represent attempts at lowering death or annihilation anxiety. Despite underlying ego deficits, on a social level these adolescents can at times be fairly appropriate. They also may appear merely neurotic, and beset with phobias, somatic symptoms and overt anxiety. The absence of an integrated sense of self, splitting, which has been defined as a lack of integration of self representations and complementary representations of the object, poor frustration tolerance, the emergence of primary process content, and temporary disintegration of thought processes and reality testing, all have been noted in studies of borderline adolescents. Borderline adolescents' potential for regression persists side by side with their potential for recompensation. Such regression is accompanied by an extreme inconsistency in relatedness and psychological functioning which, a number of authors have suggested, underscores the prevalence of splitting. This lack of integration implies that the borderline adolescent's ties to the internalized objects have been tenuous and fraught with anxiety. For the British object relations theorists, borderline adolescents' splitting has also signified the overvaluation of mental life and a preoccupation with the reality of inner objects.

Omnipotent Symbiotic and Paranoid Transference Reactions

My experience has been that many borderline adolescents retain paranoid anxiety and a magical, omnipotent symbiotic relatedness in their interactions, as well as their transference configurations. When their brief psychotic episodes occur, after an adequate process of recovery, borderline adolescents may appear to be superficially better integrated. Nevertheless, the underlying character organization, with its defenses and primitive anxiety remains basically unchanged. Evaluations of these patients conducted prior to a psychotic episode tend to reveal impulsivity together with deficits in thinking, judgment, and reality testing. Subsequent to recompensation, evaluations still show similar profiles except for improvements in reality testing and the temporary lowering of disorganizing levels of anxiety. Borderline adolescents' regressions also reveal paranoid grandiosity and the frequent use of magical thinking in symbiotic relatedness. In order to emphasize borderline adolescents' fears of annihilation and their symbiotic relatedness, I will first give a literary example before providing several vignettes which further illustrate these patients' paranoid and symbiotic transference states.

One of the most vivid portraits of a symbiotic relationship in fiction occurred in Jack London's novel, *The Call of the Wild*. The character's of the dog, Buck, and the master, Thornton, were sketched with clarity and precision. The emotional tone of the harrowing relationship between the man and the dog might be interpreted as an anxiety-laden symbiotic union of grandiose ego fragments. The plot took place in the era of gold prospecting in the Alaskan Klondike, and it focused on the idealized bond between the two after Thornton saved the dog's life. However, the protagonists' lack of ego boundaries insured their fear of mutual destruction. One of Buck's dreams recounted the annihilation anxiety inherent in pathological symbiotic attachments.

> At such times he would shake off sleep and creep through the chill to the flap of the tent, where he would stand and listen to the sound of his master's breathing...When Thornton was swept into the rapids of a stream he was trying to cross, he...held onto a rock that pulled out of the river bank. Buck dove in and...(the) current (was) behind him. Thornton reached up and closed with both arms around the shaggy neck...Buck and Thornton were jerked under the water. Strangling, suffocating, sometimes one uppermost and sometimes the other, dragging over the jagged bottom, smashing against rocks and snags, they veered into the bank... (London, 1931)

This episode from *The Call of the Wild* recalled Little's and Sullivan's descriptions of the primitive anxiety in borderline states, as well as Fairbairn's contention that pathological anxiety, associated with identification, consisted of a fear of being imprisoned and engulfed. The memorable images of this scene also metaphorically suggested several characteristics of the borderline adolescent's clinical features. The episode might have symbolized their difficulty with intrapsychic separation, the disorganizing effects of their primitive anxiety, and their grandiose use of magical thinking in symbiotic relatedness. In London's narrative voice, Buck remained the perfect, and most clever, dog in the world. Thornton, for his part, escaped any adversity as long as he was near his dog. Psychically and physically, they were inseparable, like the borderline adolescent and his internal objects. Buck, the child part of the symbiotic unit, achieved heights of heroism beyond his natural limitations. Such illusory magical powers stem from a defensive childhood omnipotence that does not dissipate because of the borderline child's simultaneous feelings of hate and fears of being annihilated. With the onset of puberty, the borderline adolescent's anxiety about annihilation, his paranoid omnipotence, and his symbiotic relatedness all impede the developmental tasks of adolescence.

Clinical evidence has shown that, in spite of their resistances and defenses against fusion, borderline adolescents frequently engage in symbiotic transference attachments. These transference states contain elements of paranoia and omnipotence in addition to the equation of both merger and separation with annihilation. I am using the term, omnipotent symbiosis, in order to convey the grandiose quality of the borderline adolescent's symbiotic relatedness. This term marks the seriously disturbed adolescent's need for absolute control over the object as a compensation for having little control over internal and external boundaries. Fairbairn (1952) juxtaposed this sense of omnipotent grandeur with the schizoid patient's efforts to dominate the inner object world. A similar term, symbiotic omnipotence, was also used by Khan (1969) with less disturbed, essentially schizoid, adult patients to refer to their demandingness and tendency to attack the analyst when their demands are unsatisfied. My work with borderline adolescents has uncovered numerous examples of both paranoid manifestations of primitive anxiety and transference attachments involving omnipotent symbiosis. It has been my impression that during such symbiotic transference states, the patient tends to experience either himself or the analyst as an omnipotent, supernatural-like force. By identifying with aspects of the adolescent patient's paranoia and omnipotence, the analyst may come to feel like either a hateful persecutor or an heroic figure. Although each of the following patients exhibited discrete psychotic signs, none suffered from prolonged episodes of psychosis. The symbiotic transference states of the patients, whom I will now describe, brought to light the extent of their defensive immersion in their own ego fragments along with their fears of annihilation.

My treatment of Frank, a thirteen year old boy, yielded abundant examples of symbiotic and paranoid relatedness.

Frank was a bright, but deeply disturbed, boy who often told me about an imaginary identical twin, whose hallucinated voice followed him everywhere. Although the twin was originally felt to be a benign presence, it criticized this patient and commanded him to attack people. Unlike truly psychotic individuals, Frank retained enough reality testing to know that the voice was imaginary, even though he acted as though it was real. During the sessions, this boy's comments about the twin were interspersed with reports of his preoccupation with violent warfare. While describing the twin's statements and his own fear of being killed at school, Frank spontaneously drew a picture of a male teenager's face. The picture consisted of a heavily shaded portrait of a teenage boy with dark sunglasses, a lit cigarette dangling from his lips, and an expression of snarling, murderous rage. My spontaneous response to this graphic depiction of suspiciousness and projected rage, was to ask Frank what I might have said or done that had indicated an intention to kill him. His fear of an omnipotent destructive power then began to emerge openly as a transference theme.

Frank experienced any frustration of his wishes as a persecution which evoked dissociated rage.   Many of his reports consisted of grandiose fantasies and rumors he had heard about gang violence and mayhem.   In the course of my inquiry during the sessions about his experience of what he perceived to be my murderous feelings, the family and interpersonal precipitants of his paranoid fantasies became clear. When Frank was less threatened by his fusion with me as a potentially violent persecutor, he began to bring his collection of gun magazines to the sessions.   His descriptions of the pictures of his favorite machine guns were told in enough loving detail to convey the he and I were being idealized, not only as twins and phallic avengers, but also as merged with the guns.   The transference fusion facilitated Frank's dealing with the primitive anxiety and the rage which surfaced whenever his defensive feelings of omnipotence were disrupted. After about a year of treatment, the hallucinated twin's disappearance coincided with much less fusion with me as a sinister, powerful force. At that point Frank demonstrated less splitting, less dissociation and less projective identification.

Chris was a withdrawn, friendless, fourteen year-old boy, with a history of strange behavior and lags in development, who was unwilling to talk about himself at all at the beginning of treatment. He did, however, volunteer to draw pictures which gradually related his fantasies. After an initial period, he shared his fantasies about several superhero-like characters, the favorite being, a wealthy playboy professional athlete who served as imaginary companion.   Through the use of fantasized telephone conversations, in which I played the part of characters that Chris invented, the transference themes became organized.   Chris eventually reported that his real identity, and mine, were alternate versions of the same person, a twenty year-old, and a fifty year-old evangelist preacher whose radio sermons were heard throughout the world. The violent thoughts of the preacher, and the radio scripts, which were elaborated in sessions, provided the means for the exploration of a symbiotic transference which reflected anxiety about hatefulness and utter disintegration. At the time that Chris began to write the scripts, he not only felt that the two of us were the same person, but also that his preaching might actually influence the world.

This patient's involvement with the fantasy characters represented a compromise solution for his hate, his omnipotence and his fear of me as an annihilating inner object. His fantasies of being the superhero and the preacher with dual identities indicated a level of grandiosity and omnipotence which were not initially interpreted.

Before elaborating on these borderline adolescents' transference reactions, I will give one additional example of symbiotic fusion in the transference.

A dangerous, deeply ill, violent fifteen year old girl, who was a patient of one of my supervisees, looked at a calendar in her therapist's office which showed a picture of a bucolic nature scene. Near the end of a session, the patient glanced at the picture on the calendar and said: "that's the Empire State Building where I was born." The patient meant this statement quite literally. Her states of symbiotic fusion and omnipotent fury could be readily understood along dynamic and defensive lines. Her expression of fusion with her therapist and the therapist's office hinted at both her fear of dissolution and her family experience. The patient apparently had felt very isolated and engulfed by an enormously cold non-human ambience. But she dreaded physical disintegration as well as annihilation of her psychic self. Many instances of her defensive symbiotic lack of differentiation from the therapist and the therapist's office occurred at the point of separations. Like the patients I have already mentioned, this girl's ego fragmentation took place in accordance with an annihilating persecutory anxiety and the dread of individuation.

Each of the borderline adolescent patients I have discussed became closely involved with the therapist or analyst in varying degrees of this kind of symbiotic transference attachment. These patients differed with respect to the extent of their paranoid and omnipotent symbiotic gestures. They all struggled with what Sullivan called the terror of disintegration, and what Winnicott identified, as the failure to reach the depressive position in maturation.

Discussion and Further
Relevant Literature

My discussion will touch only briefly on the issue of therapeutic approaches with borderline adolescents. It will more fully examine the different analytic orientations' explanations for symbiotic, paranoid transference states. The young adolescent patients, mentioned above, all displayed symbiotic relatedness and delusional perceptions of omnipotent power which allowed them to ward off their hatefulness and anxiety about annihilation. Several of these patients' ego impoverishment approached a psychotic lack of differentiation from the therapist, from other people, and from inanimate objects in the environment. They partially lost the distinction between inner and outer reality, as well as the distinction between fantasy and reality. Only a limited integrity of the body image was retained in their literal identifications with inanimate objects, such as a radioscript or a gun. Such identifications suggested both the preverbal, internalized object relations and the persecutory anxiety described by Klein, Fairbairn, Sullivan and Winnicott, and other theorists.

Beginning with early papers about body image disturbance, borderline individuals' symbiotic fusion has been discussed under a variety of conceptual headings in psychoanalytic metapsychology. Both the ego psychology Freudian model and the object relations explanations for symbiotic transference fusion derived from Freud's formulations of mental life in *The Ego and The Id*. Freud (1923) indicated that the ego was primarily, at first, a body ego and a projection of the body surface. Classical Freudian theorists, such as Schilder (1935) and Federn (1952) traced the connections between severe ego disturbance, body image distortions, and impairments in reality testing. Jacobson's (1964) combination of classical theory with an object relations orientation held that symbiotic transference states were examples of self-object fusion in psychotic identifications. Jacobson later suggested a gradation of psychotic identification in which there was a regressive dissolution of the superego. As I have already stated, according to Mahler's (1968) ego developmental theory, borderline adolescents' symbiotic relatedness was considered evidence of a developmental fixation. Borderline adolescents' states of symbiotic merger greatly resemble, what Kernberg (1975) called, the borderline patient's part object relations. According to both Kernberg's and Masterson's theoretical models, the borderline adolescent's depression and rage stem from failures to separate, and to integrate, both hated and valued parts of the self and the internal objects.

A similar phenomenon, during adulthood, has been classified by Searles (1986) as the borderline adult's dual or multiple identity processes. Searles (1960) described the instability of ego boundaries in adult borderline patients' states of nondifferentiation. He designated the extreme identity disturbance, in the borderline adult's fusion with inanimate objects, as being more typical of the schizophrenic's relationship with the non-human environment. In Searles's (1977) writings about borderline adults' impaired identity processes, he also noted that the analyst often becomes the borderline patient's symbiotic partner in the transference-countertransference. He found that borderline adults make facile use of omnipotence as a defense, particularly against what they perceive to be the horrors of empathic relatedness (Searles, 1978).

Interpersonal psychoanalysts, who were faced with the clinical material, which was mentioned above, would examine how the therapeutic interaction recreated the psychic obstacles to these patients' integration. The therapeutic inquiry in each case included a focus on the here and now interaction, and an assessment of the defensive motivation for the patients' beliefs about persecution and omnipotent power. Although Sullivan (1953) did not specifically label adolescents' signs of psychopathology as borderline phenomena, he developed extensively the ties between such adolescents' low self-esteem, their incompetence, and their impoverished interpersonal environments. In the terminology of Winnicott's (1975) object relations theory, omnipotent symbiotic transference states and psychotic disorders both reflected a false self state of ego functioning. Winnicott's model was reiterated by Modell (1968) in his attribution of borderline adolescents' symbiotic attachments to disturbances in transitional relatedness and to environmental failures. Winnicott believed that the baby controlled the transitional object in an omnipotent manner, just as the borderline patient tries to control the internalized object. According to Winnicott's model, the borderline adolescent's use of the analyst through fantasy signified healthy movement toward regression to dependence. Openness to borderline patients' symbiotic, and paranoid transference-countertransference constellations has thus been advocated under a variety of psychoanalytic rubrics.

Therapeutic Approaches

My intimation of openness to the above patients' delusional beliefs and symbiotic relatedness did not imply the use of a contrived technique. Joining these patients' fantasies, and acknowledging their destructiveness, enhanced the exploration of both their defensive omnipotence and their anxieties about inner destruction. According to Winnicott (1971), the borderline patient's object relatedness develops, as the analyst survives the patient's attacks and efforts at omnipotent control. A similar therapeutic stance was implicit in Eckstein and Wallerstein's (1957) Freudian designation of the analyst as the ally of the borderline patient's primary process. My approach of permitting the omnipotent symbiotic and paranoid transference themes to develop was somewhat similar to, what Spotnitz (1969, 1976) called, joining the narcissistic transference. Searles (1979) discussed this phenomenon as part of, what he designated as, the therapeutic symbiosis with borderline patients. When borderline patients form a therapeutic symbiosis, Searles stated, the countertransference responses affirm aspects of the delusional transference. Giovacchini (1989) termed this very same process the analyst's identification with components of the borderline patient's projected ego. Identification with borderline patients' symbiotic and paranoid feelings also reiterated Kohut's (1971, 1977) idea that, in the mirror transference, the analyst is treated as a reflection of the patients' omnipotence and grandiosity. From the vantage point of Anna Freud's theory of developmental lines, borderline adolescents' states of symbiotic fusion have been examined as a function of their disturbed relationships with the sexual body and their pre-Oedipal sexual fantasies. As I described in an earlier chapter, borderline adolescents who have been subject to full psychotic episodes have been characterized in Freudian theory as undergoing a relatively complete surrender to pregenital sexual impulses (Laufer and Laufer, 1984). A variety of interpretive approaches have been suggested, by these authors, for addressing highly disturbed adolescent's pronounced identity confusion and pregenital sexual fantasies. A wide range of therapeutic strategies with disturbed adolescents has also been offered by O. Kernberg (1979), P. Kernberg (1979), Masterson (1972), Rinsley (1980), Schimel (1992), and Sugar (1979).

Summary

The borderline adolescents, mentioned above, displayed a paranoid relatedness in which their primitive anxieties and aggressive conflicts were experienced as arising from the analyst and the external environment. All of these patients shared the young adolescent's impulsivity and dislike of introspection. As young adolescents, they had not fully negotiated the anxieties of sexual identity consolidation. They had neither attained a fully etched, overall sense of personal identity, nor come to terms with their annihilation fears and fragmentation. With all of these patients, atunement with their symbiotic identity disturbance and their omnipotent, paranoid beliefs, allowed the clinical work to proceed effectively.

An eighteen year old young man, who had borderline features, once told me with considerable excitement, that two weeks after his elderly father's death, his mother had insisted adamantly that he wear his father's trousers. The patient's automatic honoring of the request conveyed how undifferentiated he was from his mother as her symbiotic partner. His manic anxiety in telling me the story signalled his anticipation of my pleasure, as his twin, and his dead father. It simultaneously registered the fusion of ego and object which was inherent in his belief that his mother could literally read his mind and discern his thoughts and preferences.

During subsequent sessions, I gradually come to understand that this patient was letting me know that to imagine not honoring his mother's request would have felt like her death as well as his own annihilation. Behaving like one of his own ego fragments permitted the patient to avoid being flooded with primitive anxiety. Like the adolescent patients to whom I have alluded, efforts on this young man's part to form an autonomous identity involved an anxiety filled process of resolution of omnipotent destruction and untapped grief.

     In conclusion, borderline adolescents' character traits have been examined in relation to primitive anxiety about devastation of the object and the self. The preceding clinical examples highlighted defensive and maturational problems which impeded these patients' identity development. These clinical vignettes have illustrated the impact of primitive anxiety on borderline adolescents' thinking, relatedness, and defensive operations. As a consequence of their ego fragmentation, borderline adolescent patients may evoke transference-countertransference interactions in which either patient or analyst comes to feel like an idealized, undifferentiated twin, or a violent persecutor. A number of authors have emphasized borderline adult patients' splitting and merger with their own ego fragments. This chapter has given similar consideration to borderline adolescents' transferential recreation of their infantile object relationships.

CHAPTER EIGHT

HOMICIDAL ADOLESCENTS

Even where it emerges without any sexual purpose, in the blindest fury of destructiveness, the satisfaction of an instinct is accompanied by an extraordinarily high degree of narcissistic enjoyment...owing to its old wishes for omnipotence.

Sigmund Freud

Psychoanalytic perspectives on violent, antisocial adolescents' character trends have had much to offer treatment programs. Fervent concern about homicidal adolescents has been reflected in attempts to understand their character disturbance from both developmental and psychodynamic points of view. In *The Ego and the Id*, Freud (1923) related criminal behavior in youths to an unbearable sense of unconscious guilt which was primarily Oedipal in origin. He later stated in his preface to Aichhorn's (1935) *Wayward Youth* that neither juvenile delinquents, nor criminals had the fully developed psychic apparatus which was essential for psychoanalysis. Glover (1956, 1960) defined delinquents' criminal behavior as a series of hostile attacks on the environment which were motivated by a powerful unconscious need for punishment. According to these dynamic formulations about antisocial youth, homicidal assaults entailed an attack on unrecognized persecutors, a mechanism for the alleviation of guilt, and repressed wishes for punishment.

Assessments of the characterological features and the internalized object relations of extremely violent youth have been employed to a powerful effect. One important psychoanalytic portrait of youthful criminal behavior, by Redl (1951), stressed anal character traits which involved a spiteful rejection of societal norms and diminished superego control over id-derived antisocial activities. Bowlby (1953) found that prolonged separation from the mother, during the first years of life, was the primary cause of delinquent, antisocial character trends. In Kernberg's (1975) dichotomy of the character disorders, violent, antisocial personalities were classified as low level character disorders with underlying borderline personality organization. Psychopathic personalities were considered to be a subgroup of the narcissistic disorders. Such inquiries have been essential for establishing treatment parameters. But aside from the influence of the abusive family and the sociocultural milieu, what psychic factors predispose disturbed adolescents to overtly express murderous rage? What role can individual treatment play in reducing the possibilities that adolescents, who have maimed or killed, will commit further acts of violence? This chapter will review psychoanalytic studies which have shed light on these issues while focusing on early object relations phenomena. I will hypothesize that the relationship between narcissism and paranoia in violent, antisocial adolescents has particular relevance to their treatment needs.

Introduction

My area of emphasis in this chapter will be the intrapsychic and characterological aspects of extreme violence. My initial objective will be to summarize the clinical features and the range of homicidal adolescent's psychopathology. Many psychoanalytic writers have confirmed the role of family dynamics in homicidal adolescents' violent assaults (Easson, 1961; Sargent, 1965). Even though adolescents' acts of explosive aggression cannot be exclusively associated with family violence and abuse, a large number of homicidal youths come from abusive, violent families. The prevalence of conscious and unconscious, disguised parental messages to adolescents to express themselves through violence, represented one such consideration, which followed from Reiner and Kaufman's (1959) conception of character disorders in adolescence. In addition, the violent actions of antisocial adolescents have been described in theory, as diminishing the threats of internalized persecutors, while restoring an illusory infantile omnipotence. As a synthesis of the theoretical views of Eissler, Greenacre, Kohut, and Winnicott, I wish to stress the paranoid, narcissistic character trends of homicidal adolescents. Homicidal adolescents' sadistic fantasies of erotized aggression, their infantile rage, and their need for continuous revenge against projected internalized persecutors all suggest the characteristics of a narcissistic, paranoid character style.

Clinical Features

Although a preponderance of psychotic, and psychopathic traits occur in many children and adolescents who have killed, underlying narcissistic, and paranoid characterological features should be a focus of treatment. Based on the work of Kohut and Winnicott, violent assaults by antisocial youth can be seen as serving essentially narcissistic functions in two ways. First, their rage tends to be discharged against an internalized fused self-object image. Second, the defensive role of dehumanization and sadistic fantasies must be considered in light of these adolescents' ego limitations and persistent hypervigilance. Sadistic fantasies have been described by both Winnicott and Kohut as having a narcissistic origin. Such fantasies commonly persist among homicidal adolescents whose expressions of annihilating rage seemingly restore them to a state of infantile omnipotence. Furthermore, intensely violent adolescents' lack of concern for their victims results not simply from psychopathic indifference, but from a dehumanization of the victim as object. Homicidal adolescents vent rage at fused self-object images of internalized persecutors, which grow more threatening, with misperceived slights to their self-esteem. I wish to suggest that their sadistic fantasies and explosively violent assaults can be understood as involving paranoid attempts at the redress of an underlying narcissistic vulnerability. Their exciting fantasies of murder and mayhem serve as the basis for a paranoid repertory of defensive denials of primitive anxiety.

The combined effects, on adolescents, of pathological parent-child interactions, and organically based developmental deficits, were first described by Bender (1940, 1953, 1959, 1974) in a number of in-depth investigations of hospitalized children and adolescents who committed murder. In one study of severe aggression, and hostility, in children, Bender commented on the frequency of such youngsters' intense rivalry and competition for parental attention. In a review of thirty four histories of hospitalized children who had killed, she noted severe early deprivation, schizophrenic signs in many of the patients, and a general absence of guilt or remorse. These children reportedly saw their homicidal acts as having been accidental, unexpected, or unintentionally fatal. Bender attributed their homicidal behavior to the disorganizing effect of environmental factors on patterned drive control. Among these groups of hospitalized patients were psychopathic children who were characteristically aggressive and lacking in anxiety. Because they were deficient in the capacity for identification, or object love, owing to the lack of an early relationship with a love object, their aggression was of a diffuse nature. Their victims were experienced as having little value or meaning. Within the framework of a behavioral approach, adolescents' violent aggression has also been considered to be a learned response to the frustration of nurturance and dependency needs (Bandura, 1959). In an earlier study of children who killed, Bender disclosed the presence of signs of organic brain disease, epilepsy, and schizophrenia. In a similar vein, Lewis (1983, 1985) and others have pointed to possible neurological impairments in many homicidal adolescents. Nevertheless, deprivation, abuse, and rejections provide the early framework for paranoid defenses and narcissistic disturbances in homicidal adolescents, which are compounded by the later fusion of their erotic and destructive impulses.

Narcissistic Disturbance and Sadistic Fantasies

Among homicidal adolescents, the grandiosity of early childhood narcissism does not become tempered with empathy, or transformed into an appropriate ability to maintain realistic self- appraisals. The body of Kohut's work was adept at revealing narcissistic youths' vacillations between states of grandiosity and feelings of helplessness and inadequacy. Berkowitz and associates (1974) attributed wide fluctuations in self-esteem in adolescents, with narcissistic trends, to an underlying narcissistic vulnerability. They hypothesized that the essence of such adolescents' narcissistic disturbances stemmed from the lack of an internal system for self-esteem regulation. Data analysis of repeated interviews and family therapy sessions provided firm clinical evidence that the parents they studied used their narcissistic adolescent children as objects for the regulation of their own tenuous self-esteem. The self of each of these adolescents remained a continuous interlocking system, between parent and child, which fostered the maintenance of a precarious narcissistic equilibrium. Adolescents who have grown up in such family constellations remain aggressively tied to fulfilling and rebelling against parental expectations, and dependent on their parents for their own fragile self-esteem. Such adolescents demonstrate great difficultly in undergoing the separation tasks of adolescence and in acquiring an autonomous identity. A number of authors have also highlighted the central dynamic importance of revenge and rage in adolescents' narcissistic character trends.   This theme - the pervasiveness of narcissistic rage-had been previously discussed by Kohut (1966, 1968, 1971), in terms of fundamental self-esteem problems.

As an extension of both Kohut's and Winnicott's views, it has been my impression that antisocial adolescents who kill are not merely lacking in impulse control, acting out an Oedipal hatred, or expressing poorly controlled rage. They tend to be characterized by both paranoid trends, and a vengeful, narcissistic rage. Their narcissistic rage is expressed through violent attacks on symbolic representations of a poorly integrated part-self-object. Because of the confluence of paranoid and narcissistic disturbances, homicidal adolescents may be able to feel less threatened, and more instinctually alive, when enacting destructive, sadistic fantasies. Winnicott (1975) maintained that the erotization of aggression can be a cause of compulsive sadistic tendencies in narcissistic personalities. Similarly, in Klein's (1930) elaboration of early ego development, she noted the undeveloped ego's incapacity to master primitive, sadistic anxiety. According to Kohut (1972), violent forms of narcissistic rage arose in individuals who needed total control over an infantile environment. In Kohut's theory, this need for absolute control was essential because of either the unavailability of the admiring selfobject, or the lack of opportunity for merger with an idealized object. The unavailability, for the mirroring process, of abusive, rejecting parents has been well-documented. There has been a consensus, in theory, that homicidal adolescents' acts of violent aggression, represent not only paranoid expressions of rage, but also, a simultaneous defensive response to injured self-esteem, and a sadistic attempt to repair the self through revenge.   In addition, violent acts, by narcissistically vulnerable, paranoid youths, involve attempts at the unconscious resolution of trauma in early object relations which are perpetuated by subsequent family transactions.

Reich (1960) expanded Freud's work by defining early disturbances in narcissism which occurred before self-object differentiation. Such disturbances were characterized, by Reich, as resulting in an impaired capacity for self-esteem regulation and failures in empathy. In tracing the growth of healthy self-esteem, Kohut, like Sullivan, subsequently stressed the importance of parents' availability for the self-enhancing mirroring process. Kohut reasoned that traumatic interferences with this process resulted in narcissistic rage which involved both the need for revenge, and the persistent compulsion to pursue it. Narcissistic rage encompassed a total lack of empathy and an intense need to blot out any offense which was directed against the grandiose self. Bach and Schwartz (1972) made use of Kohut's theories in reaching their conclusion that the omnipotence and grandiosity of the injured infantile self can be reaffirmed through sadistic fantasies. In these authors' analysis of elaborately violent fantasies, like those of the Marquis de Sade, several findings were noteworthy. They suggested that rage, subsequent to an insult to the grandiose self, had a pervasive tendency to linger. Its retaliatory nature was often directed against a depriving mother image, and feelings of anxiety, helplessness, and inadequacy accompanied the rage. Such feelings, in turn, tended to necessitate further reparation for lost self-esteem. Moreover, in Freudian theory, the traumatized adolescent male has been described in terms of an aggressivization of the penis, and an erotization of the whole body (Reich, 1960). Most homicidal, or severely violent, antisocial adolescents are male.

Homicidal adolescents enact violent, sadistic fantasies as they fluctuate in self-regard between blithe omnipotence and fiercely dissociated feelings of inadequacy. Sexuality and aggression become merged with their paranoid, narcissistic need for revenge. One such youth may fantasize about violent fights and beatings, whereas another will be preoccupied with predatory fantasies about people being mutilated and bleeding. Stolorow (1975) believed that, in sadomasochistic relationships, the sadist gains narcissistic satisfaction through an identification with the pain of the victim and a sense of omnipotent control over the victim. These same dynamic processes hold true for homicidal, antisocial adolescents. Their expression of annihilating rage restores the illusion of an infantile grandiosity through the fragile reacquisition of a sense of omnipotent power.

This pervasive, sadistic need for absolute control, by inflicting pain, was illustrated by a twenty one year old former member of a violent street gang who told me about a conversation with his usually, passive, very pregnant girlfriend. When she disagreed with him by raising an objection to his obnoxious demands, he erupted in a violent rage while yelling: "You're never too pregnant to be slapped". This patient's need for revenge coincided with his need for restoration of infantile omnipotence. The combination of these needs, with his paranoid orientation, had created a disposition for ego syntonic expressions of fury and violence. The detached, amorphous quality of this man's relatedness stood in marked contrast to the triumphant exhilaration he felt during his contemptuous, aggressive outbursts. His extravagant indifference to others' feelings, and his arrogant rages, maintained a level of grandiosity which is one of the hallmarks of the psychopathic, narcissistic personality.

When Freud alluded to the narcissistic enjoyment of destructiveness, he paved the way for the scrutiny of the dynamic and structural relationships between violent acts and narcissistic character traits.

Ego Deficits, Dehumanization, and Paranoia

The cognitive limitations and paranoid trends of delinquent adolescents, in general, and homicidal adolescents, in particular, have been explored by a variety of investigators (Johnson and Szurek, 1952; Toch, 1969). In a psychoanalytic account of violent gang members, Spiegel (1972) concluded that violence was a form of communication for these adolescents, who showed characteristic deficits in vocabulary, abstraction and verbal imagery. Their dreams contained numerous, matter of fact, violent assaults, without symbolic disguise, in which there were both thrill seeking aspects, and violent escapes from danger. A similar appreciation of delinquent adolescents' ego and cognitive deficits emerged in the work of Greenacre (1950) and Blos (1971). Both of these authors posited that, for the violent delinquent, a predisposition for acting out existed in the distorted relationship of action to speech and thought. A selective superego deficit was common, in these antisocial youths, together with a characteristic dependence on action as a replacement for verbalized thought. Greenacre also depicted delinquents' acting-out in terms of manifest versus latent action themes. The latent meaning of their violent actions symbolically represented their constricted affective experience. These antisocial adolescents' expressions of conflict through action, or violence, became a substitute for their meager, mental organization of experience.

Adolescents' reliance on action has been closely tied to their difficulty with problem solving, and their concretization of thought. On an object-relations level, Greenacre reported a primitive continuation of partial objects. Rather than struggle with the nuances of frustration and conflict, the delinquent adolescents, she evaluated, typically relied on violent acts. The environment became, for them, merely a medium for tension regulation, and other people were reduced to sources of need satisfaction. The violent actions of homicidal adolescents can, likewise, be seen as having defensive components. Such adolescents demonstrate prelogical thinking and the tendency to act out, rather than to reflect, assimilate, and respond. Vacillations in their self-esteem, and limitations in their object relations development, contribute to making their violence ego-syntonic.

An attempt, by Miller and Looney (1974), to categorize clinical syndromes among homicidal adolescents highlighted these adolescents' episodic loss of control, and their sadistic tendency to dehumanize their victims. Menninger had (1956) first introduced the concept of episodic dyscontrol, which he defined, as momentary, marked lapses of control, which inhibit further decompensation in a disintegrating personality structure. Dehumanization involves a pathological projection of some split-off, unacceptable aspect of the self onto the other. When dehumanization occurs, reality testing suffers to some degree, and the victim, who may represent an image of the internalized depriving object, loses his or her humanity.

According to Miller and Looney, the most dangerous violent adolescents were either, first, those who were subject to marked episodic dyscontrol, who also showed total dehumanization of their victims, or, second, those who showed partial dehumanization, along with an aggressive eroticization of part objects. The former group of adolescent murderers were narcissistic, omnipotent personalities for whom violence was ego-syntonic. The capacity for dehumanization was the feature which distinguished these adolescents from merely, assaultive adolescents. Homicidal adolescents who belong to lower risk groups have been characterized, in both theory and research, as requiring support and encouragement from external sources - i.e., the youth gang - in order to kill. Shatan (1977), likewise, emphasized the key roles of the erotization of killing and systematic dehumanization in the group socialization process inherent in basic combat training. Most of the adolescents, whom the above authors studied, revealed routine, sadistic, erotic fantasies which clearly indicated a mixture of sexual arousal and murderous aggression.

The notion of homicidal violence, as a defense against further ego-disruption, has been emphasized by many writers who concluded that adolescents who killed, impulsively, without any apparent motive, often did not have a prior history of serious aggressive, antisocial acts, (Blackman, 1963; Reichard, 1950). Blackman assembled a personality profile of schizoid, and borderline male killers, with a weak masculine sexual identification, who were easily provoked into rage. The murders, which these youths committed, followed periods of profound struggles against dependency longings, and feelings of helplessness, which added to the threat of impeding psychotic episodes.

In another detailed investigation of adolescents' homicides, Smith (1965) examined adolescent killers, ranging from age fourteen to twenty one, and uncovered a pattern of ego weakness and a susceptibility to episodic loss of control. These adolescents' profiles all suggested a character organization which was traceable to early deprivation. Their histories revealed oral incorporation fantasies and an infantile clinging to love objects, as well as severe disruptions in family relationships. The emotional unavailability of the parents of homicidal adolescents intensifies these youngsters' ego and superego deficits. The diminished superego of the violent, antisocial adolescent allows for marked eruptions of rage, and limitations in avenues for its expression. When disappointment or frustration unleashes a primitive infantile rage a sudden loss of ego-object differentiation may occur. The conclusions and overall clinical results of many authors (Blackman, Miller and Looney, and Smith) have supported Eissler's (1950) psychoanalytic view that homicidal aggression arises from anxiety and panic in the delinquent adolescent. Bromberg (1971) mentioned the related point, with which I am in agreement, that homicide represents a multidetermined response to the adolescent's anxiety about being destroyed. Such anxieties occur in accord with both an underlying infantile omnipotence, and erotized aggression, as Kohut and Winnicott hypothesized.

The need to attack, in order to defend against projected physical and psychic assaults, generally characterizes homicidal adolescents, as well as other groups of adolescents with paranoid character disturbance whose early life has exposed them to violence and abuse. As I mentioned in Chapter Three, abused adolescents, especially, make inappropriate attributions of hostility. Paranoid propensities for extreme hypersensitivity to feeling slighted, and the deficient ability to trust, are also compounded in the homicidal adolescent by impaired introspection ability. These adolescents' expressions of homicidal rage momentarily keep in check the threat of their feeling helpless and humiliated. On the basis of a great deal of clinical experience with violent drug addicts, Lefer (1984) dissected the prevalence of this hypervigilant, paranoid, almost guard dog-like, mental state in which violent assaults required the inflicting of pain, and punishment, for repressed injuries. Lefer found frequent examples of this paranoid cognitive set among ex-convicts who had killed and mutilated people, and he believed that the extremely violent youth lacks human bonds to the point of needing to inflict pain in order to feel visible and worthwhile. During adolescence, violent youths may turn to gangs which support their faltering sense of identity through drug use, gun possession and violent acts. Homicidal adolescents' paranoid needs to punish and to inflict pain are solidified by grandiosity which is fuelled by their identifications with group violence and exaggerated images of hypermasculine predators.

Case Material

Several examples of psychopathic, homicidal behavior and paranoid, narcissistic character disturbance have been brought to my attention by psychotherapists during supervision. Predatory aggression, the lack of empathy and primitive object relations have all been found to be widespread among grotesquely violent young adults (Meloy, 1988).

A seventeen year old girl, who had been physically abused as a child, stabbed her grandmother to death, in spite of a course of lengthy psychotherapy for her violent, assaultive behavior. This girl showed no overt symptoms of psychosis or borderline trends, but she exhibited psychopathic features, and had a long history of paranoid ideation and antisocial behavior. She was subject to feelings of inferiority and narcissistic rage, to which she responded, by assaultive behavior with little or no overt provocation. In spite of her meager musical and vocal talents, and her limited reading ability, she often became lost in fantasies about performing as a world-famous entertainer. Dehumanization and the potential for violent acting out were combined with her shallow affect and a volatile, narcissistic relatedness.

This patient's self-esteem had been enhanced, prior to the killing, by her frequently carrying weapons and by encouraging her friends to engage in hostile, aggressive actions. Her productions during therapy showed an ego-syntonic need for violent behavior, a complete lack of concern for the consequences of her actions, and a pervasive, poorly controlled rage.

A narcissistic, eighteen year old boy, who harbored nearly constant rage, experienced no remorse after committing homicide. He beat an elderly man to death on the street after a minor argument in which the man criticized him. Neglected, overindulged and isolated throughout his early childhood, this boy became highly aggressive, and socially provocative, after puberty. He feared both men and women, and his fears stemmed from projected fears of his own demandingness and rage. Yet, his dependency longings had been deeply repressed, and they threatened his defensive composure. This patient's need to maintain and protect positive, idealized parental images played a dynamic role in his denied depression and his outbursts of aggressive behavior. Whenever he felt slighted or insulted, his urge to express violent aggressive feelings became overwhelming. The anonymous man's criticism dealt a severe blow to his self-esteem, and it became the stimulus for a retaliation against an unconscious combined image of himself and his internalized tormentors.

During less-defended moments with his therapist, this boy volunteered his characteristic fantasies, which contained omnipotent, sadistic themes, of his victims jumping out of windows, and women being raped and stabbed. This patient's narcissistic psychopathy, his dehumanization and his paranoid level of suspiciousness presented grave barriers to emotional growth, and to his involvement in a therapeutic relationship. Both of these adolescents came from neglectful, abusive families. Included among their dominant character trends were: dehumanization, paranoid anxiety, the absence of either empathy or a sophisticated morality, and narcissistic rage which escalated into gratuitous violence.

Treatment Issues

Beginning with Aichhorn's (1935) discovery of the narcissistic transference in delinquent youth, psychoanalytic clinicians have suggested that, with a suitable environment, violent, antisocial adolescents' fragile self-esteem may present the possibility of a therapeutic strategy. Aichhorn urged that therapists confront delinquent youths by providing a mirror image of their grandiosity in the hope of developing a therapeutic alliance. Clinical experience with severely violent, homicidal adolescents, suggests that, when these adolescents receive individual insight-oriented treatment, the structured milieu of a hospital, or a residential treatment center remains essential for addressing their infantile object relations and pathological defenses. The structure which is provided by hospitalization or residential treatment may provide homicidal adolescents with the external controls which are needed for their maturation. The combination of systematic limit setting and support which is offered within a structured therapeutic milieu offers hope for dealing with homicidal adolescents' infantile needs, their grandiosity and their hypersensitivity. Such settings provide clinicians with a measure of needed safety from these patient's rages and their frequent distortions of interpersonal interactions.

Although psychoanalytic psychotherapy has generally not been advocated with extremely violent delinquents, it has been tried successfully with some parameters. Eissler recommended the establishment of a preparatory phase of treatment, which had as its principal goal, the development of a meaningful transference relationship. Eissler (1950) also emphasized that:

> the predominantly narcissistic quality of the delinquent's personality, his incapacity of loving..... and the consequent absence of any spontaneous positive transference reaction, make it necessary that the analyst provoke or create the positive transference by active measures.

From this point of view, the violent delinquent may develop a transference attachment, when the analyst has been experienced as an omnipotent being who is consistently interested in the patient's benefit. Such an impression emerges as a result of the analyst's ability to respond to hateful devaluations, interpretatively, without hateful retaliations.

Effective clinical work rests on the ability to appropriately confront to the homicidal adolescent's hostility, without tolerating being the victim of abusive attacks. In spite of their guarded prognosis, impulse-ridden, antisocial adolescents' characterological features suggest the importance of a challenging, limit setting approach.   The integration of a more-cohesive sense of self, and the development of relatedness, empathy and impulse control remain crucial treatment goals for homicidal adolescents. These patients' infantile lapses of impulse control, their paranoid mistrust, and their frenzied flights from persecutory objects, all magnify the difficulties of establishing a therapeutic alliance.

The need to address underlying paranoid and narcissistic character trends is paramount. The involvement of family members, in family therapy, may provide an opportunity for some alteration of the interpersonal environment within which the paranoid, narcissistic disturbances have been perpetuated. The potential for future violent behavior can be reduced, if homicidal adolescents enhance their capacities for controlled expressions of anger and rage, while developing less pathological self-esteem and more healthy relatedness.   Spotnitz (1964, 1979) discussed extensively the use of techniques which mobilized such rage in the transference, particularly paradigmatic techniques, which minimized   the   patient's   expression   of   rage   in   actions. Countertransference problems with homicidal adolescents are intensified by the negative reactions they evoke, by therapists' anxiety about their own aggression, as well as by concerns for personal safety.   These patients' primitive defenses, their intolerance for frustration, and their cognitive deficits all strengthen their ideas of reference and their grandiose, narcissistic tendencies.

By assessing adult killers' underlying object representations of their victims, Meloy (1988) was able to offer tentative hypotheses about the relationship between diagnosis and psychotherapy outcome. Hospitalized adult killers with borderline personality disorders showed the best prognosis while those with the worst prognosis had both psychotic and psychopathic features.   Lefer (1984) observed that an interest in the violence-prone person's dreams and childhood memories elicited clinging behavior and strong positive transference attachments.   On the basis of his treatment of institutionalized, violent delinquents, Marohn (1981) focused on both the negative transference, and the difficulty these patients had with the identification and expression of internal states.   In an unpublished study of the hospital course and treatment of ten adolescents who killed, D. Winn (1975) reported clinical improvement in their overt symptomatology but little characterological change.   Winn found that these adolescents exhibited a generalized lack of concern for their victims, together with a fear of punishment rather than remorse or guilt. Homicidal adolescents' regressed object relations and paranoid character traits present marked obstacles to therapeutic progress. Nevertheless, the combination of individual and group therapy remains clinically useful for addressing these patients' pathological use of projection, and their other defensive processes.

Summary

Paranoid and narcissistic character features, particularly self-esteem disturbances and narcissistic rage, underlie the psychodynamics of antisocial adolescents' homicidal behavior. Adolescents' homicidal assaults are facilitated by the presence of dehumanization, by paranoid losses of impulse control and by eroticized, sadistic fantasies. Homicidal youths' lack of concern for their victims, and their preoccupations with violence, have been explained on the basis of such characterological factors. Psychoanalytic studies of treatment, with very violent adolescents, have highlighted to the efficacy of a dual therapeutic focus on the evocation of their infantile narcissism, and their paranoid mistrust, within a secure environment. The extremely violent adolescent's evolving capacity for relatedness, and empathy, depends upon the emergence of his ability to develop empathy for himself. Whether through a transference attachment, or simple respect for the therapist's ability to set limits without hateful retaliations, the homicidal adolescent faces the task of relinquishing illusory omnipotence and acquiring self-awareness in light of cognitive deficits and widespread ego impairments. Homicidal adolescent patients need the most secure settings in order to come to terms with their repressed fears of annihilation and their status as infantile, impulsive slaves of internalized persecutors.

CHAPTER NINE

Adolescents' Identity Disturbance And Acting Out

I did not know what "myself" was, sexuality (even if known) was totally irrelevant and meaningless unless existence and survival could be taken for granted, and personal identity established.

Margaret Little

In Freud's (1914) writings, acting out referred to enactments of sexual and aggressive conflicts, as well as to a form of resistance to the psychoanalytic procedure. Acting out typifies disturbed adolescents' defensive efforts to shun depression and separation anxiety, in addition to anxiety about their lack of a differentiated sense of identity. During adolescence, the sense of personal identity reflects psychic discontinuities which are a matter of degree, rather than all or none phenomena. Healthy adolescents depend on dreams and fantasies to express the anxieties inherent in identity differentiation and consolidation. Poorly integrated adolescents routinely enact these anxieties, as they recreate their object relations problems, interpersonally.

Adolescent's struggles with acceptance of their sexuality, their uncertainties about intimacy, and their lack of a realistic time perspective, all compound their difficulties with individuation from internal objects in pursuit of a more fully developed sense of personal identity. Adolescents with marked antisocial and borderline trends typically experience instances of identity fragmentation which are exacerberated by unconscious pressures to act out form the family system. While the child play acts a repetition of affectively changed experience in order to attain mastery, adolescents with severe character pathology recreate symbolic expressions of identity disturbance without achieving further integration. Having traced borderline, psychotic and homicidal adolescents' lack of identity integration and their primitive anxiety states, I will now explore the overall subject of adolescents' identity disturbance, and in particular, the defensive aspects of the disturbed adolescent's use of movement and antisocial actions.

Introduction

This chapter will include only a limited examination of the topic of identity disturbance. It will focus more fully on the psychodynamic linkage between movement and persistent acting out tendencies. Movement has particular relevance for adolescent psychological development, because action and acting-out behaviors are so closely related. I am not using the term, acting out, in its fully technical sense, but rather, to signify impulsive enactments of internal conflict. As an integration of the Freudian, interpersonal and object relations theories of development, I will offer the proposition that both healthy and severely ill adolescents inevitably involve movement in countering the depressive moods and the spectrum of separation anxieties which accompany identity integration. My hypothesis will be that movement play, and explosions of acting out, retain their object relational aspects throughout adolescence. Unlike antisocial, borderline and other disturbed youths who persist in their acting out behavioral enactments, relatively healthy adolescents rely on movement play and fantasies to negotiate primitive anxieties and identity consolidation.

It has been my observation that adolescents' movement and locomotion fantasies yield considerable data about their identity strivings. Physical activities and movement fantasies enter into adolescents' attempts to counteract intense anxieties about mourning and annihilation. Identity loss is typically expressed in adolescents' antisocial behavior. The impulsive actions of the adolescent with severe character disturbance lack the creativity and the imaginative dialogues with internalized objects, which are expressed in healthy children's play. Nevertheless, chronically acting out adolescents' behavior problems are with unconscious counterphobic responses to primitive anxieties which reflect identity loss. Young adolescents with severe conduct disturbance depend greatly on defensive acting out. Older adolescents with antisocial and borderline features often rely on immediate action as the principal avenue for the expression of their primitive anxieties.

Identity Formation
And
Locomotion

Phenomenologically, identity refers to the psychological state of being and remaining oneself. Identity disturbance encompasses a self-estrangement continuum, which ranges from neurotic anxiety and self-consciousness, to more primitive anxiety, depersonalization, and the relinquishment of ego and body boundaries. Erikson (1959, 1968), characterized identity formation during adolescence as a simultaneous process of individuation and changes in values, self images, and ego functions which include societal influences. Reports of instances of severe identity loss, (by Fairbairn, A. Freud, Fromm, Klein, Little, Searles, Sullivan, and Winnicott), have connected its subjective aspects to primitive anxiety, ego dedifferentiation and fears of annihilation. The unconscious terror of identity may loss become immobilizing as adolescents alternate between indifferent avoidance and obsessive concern with symbolic expressions of identity elements. The adolescent who experiences severe identity loss fails to perceive himself as either autonomous, or as a continuous, integrated physical presence in time and space. Adolescents' fleeting depressions stem, in part, from unrecognized insecurity about remaining themselves, and from a lack of tolerance for the anxiety which accompanies physical change, character and identity reorganization.

Locomotion - the ability to move and to walk - allows the child to put into action the object relations aspects of the intrapsychic separation process. Motility, an early ego function, is usually the term designated for the phenomena which will be considered here. Yet, the term, locomotion, seems more appropriate for the present purpose. It connotes the effects on the object and the self of the capacity to walk and to manipulate the environment. Locomotion and the identity sense are closely allied from early childhood through adolescence. During early childhood, movement becomes central to the expression of anxiety about separateness and to the resolution of inner object tensions. Ambivalent efforts at individuation, as well as separation anxieties are expressed in movement fantasies and games. Such fantasies extend from childhood into the acting out behaviors of adolescence and early adulthood.

Young children use movement to practice separation and to undo anxiety about differentiation from their parents. Greenacre, Jacobson,

Mahler, and Winnicott all suggested that considerable growth in the body image, and body awareness, accompanies the young child's efforts to distinguish self representations from object representations. From the perspective of Sullivan's interpersonal theory, walking allows the emerging self to be experienced as separate, active, and competent, at least to some extent. Walking makes possible the child's relating to the mother at varying physical distances, and it facilitates opportunities for having an increasing impact on the physical, and interpersonal environment. The one to two and half year old child's excitement in autonomy and mastery is revealed in the exuberant pleasures of crawling, climbing, running, jumping, leaping, swinging, and hanging upside down. While the toddler epistemologist fancies that *I know that I am me because I am moving,* the teenage metaphysician maintains that *I know that I am me, because I can change my image.* From the toddler's activities as a starting point, children employ movement play with the body, as well as with toys, to experiment with intrapsychic separateness and individuation.

My proposed formulation of these tendencies has arisen from clinical observations about a number of child and adolescent patients.

> A seven year old girl, whom I saw in play therapy for severe phobias, and conduct problems, spent much of her time in sessions placing a small doll in a toy airplane. The plane's flights returned ritualistically to precisely the same spot on the playroom floor. An eleven year old girl, who was antisocial and quite ill, ruminated at home and in her sessions about subway car details to the point of excluding almost all other subjects from consciousness. A fifteen year old boy, with both antisocial and borderline traits, reported to me that he spent most of his free time riding the New York City subways without ever setting a destination. These patients' rituals conveyed their fears about remaining either integrated, or functionally competent, when alone. All three patients demonstrated a diffuse, poorly differentiated sense of personal identity.

Very disturbed children's repetitive movement play during treatment sessions expresses unconscious anxieties about fusion, and the eradication of ego boundaries, which are often experienced in the transference.

The fifteen year old boy's subway rides mitigated his primitive terror of both leaving and returning to his domineering parents, on whom he felt utterly dependent. It was usually only his journeys to my office that led to a specific destination. Since he rarely arrived at any definite destination, he seemed to reduce the fear that he might attain a threatening degree of differentiation. Yet, he did travel on his own. The subway trips provided this patient with an action-oriented defensive maneuver which meshed with his compulsive character. The enactment of his locomotion fantasies and identity disturbance transformed his anxiety about annihilation, and disintegration, into a dialogue between the undifferentiated self, at the home station, and the partially differentiated self which was able to travel. Like adolescents' reliance on acting out, childrens' preoccupations with movement play suggest counterphobic reversals of fears of both the loss of the object and the loss of the self (Eckstein and Friedman, 1957; Fraiberg, 1969).

Adolescents' fantasies and dreams, about trips and vehicles, renew separation anxiety themes inherent in the young child's locomotion fantasies and games. The adolescent, who dreams, such dreams, expresses concern about identity integrity and the competence of the individuating self. Locomotion dreams thus combine psychodynamic material with the dreamer's anxiety about psychic survival. Relatively healthy adolescents' dreams and movement fantasies express their latent separation anxiety, without identity loss or dangerous and self-injurious behavior. However, periods of anxiety and depression must be endured, at least temporarily, by the adolescent for a successful negotiation of identity consolidation and individuation (Blos, 1962; Erikson, 1968; Jacobson, 1964). Although adolescents with severe character pathology and healthy adolescents share the anguish of this life phase, they bring to the developmental tasks of adolescence, different characterological tendencies and different levels of maturity in object relations and ego integrity.

Movement Play, Affect and Separation Anxiety

Oscar Wilde once observed that self-love is the beginning of a lifelong romance. Parents' enjoyment of the young child's burgeoning relatedness and locomotion skills lends this love affair much of its original magic. From infancy on, locomotion is associated with the child's anxieties about object loss and with the growing sense of autonomy. In *Beyond the Pleasure Principle,* Freud (1920) depicted his 18-month-old grandson's game of throwing small objects under the bed. In one variation, a cotton reel, which was attached to a piece of string, was tossed forward and then enthusiastically pulled backwards. Freud considered separation anxiety to be the prototype of all later anxieties, and he concluded that his grandson's game dealt with acceptance versus protest of separation from his mother. In Freud's formulation, it was precisely through movement play that young children manifested the elation of autonomy and the fear of separation. Research investigations of locomotion and emotional development confirmed Freud's suggestion that babies, and toddlers, rely heavily on motility to express affective states (Gesell and Amatruda 1941). Locomotion also greatly facilitates the evolution of the two year old's aggressive and oppositional behaviors. According to Freudian theory, locomotion entails either defensive strategies, or substitutions for the child's expression of sexual and aggressive impulses (Mittlemann, 1954, 1955). As locomotion becomes intertwined with motivational systems, movement is connected with increasing ego organization and libidinal conflicts. In fact, fantasies, dreams and games, involving motor activity, potentially symbolize the full gamut of psychosexual anxieties and conflicts.

The three-year-old riding a tricycle, the seven-year old riding a bicycle, and the 17-year-old driving a first car all may exhibit anxiety about separation and autonomous functioning. Proficiency at motor tasks contributes to their self-confidence, and the combination of the two, sets a positive emotional tone for the increasing separations from the home and family. Children, who are in treatment, likewise, use movement and vehicle toys to practice separation and to test the accuracy of good and bad self and parental images. Autonomy and physical prowess remain particularly important for the adolescent, who undergoes the stresses of body image consolidation and differentiation, together with the psychological preparation for actually leaving home (Geleerd, 1961). The adolescent's progress with individuation, and his or her efforts at securing an integrated identity, can be gauged by the nature of locomotion themes in fantasy, in play, and in interpersonal encounters.

Locomotion serves multiple functions for the child by fostering growth in defensive processes, body boundaries, and reality testing (Kanzer, 1957). The ability to approach and avoid others by motor activity allows for physical manifestations of a flight for internalized relationships. From an object relations standpoint, locomotion fantasies and play express transitional states which have been characterized as being crucial to development (Winnicott, 1951, 1971). Winnicott defined transitional play as a maturationally significant, imaginative blurring of the distinction between external reality and the child's inner world. Movement play, which has transitional qualities, executes the young child's ability to maintain contact with the internalized mother, while exercising separate ego functions.

A number of Freudian theorists who share a developmental orientation have stressed the cognitive and affective growth accompanying locomotion. Locomotion has been described in Freudian theory as reducing castration anxiety, as well as anxiety about the dissolution of body boundaries. In addition, locomotion augments the child's growing sense of reality by permitting physical exploration of the real world. When the one to two year old child is able to walk about freely, omnipotence and magical fantasies can be more subject to reality testing. Locomotion also adds to the child's perception of body sensations as one's own. At first, vision, hearing, and touch increase the child's awareness of the body, and the differentiation of the self from mother, but later locomotion increases body exhibitionism and self differentiation. Mahler's (1958) research described upright locomotion as a developmental landmark in identity formation. Greenacre (1958) noted that increased physical contact with the world led to a generalized libidinal investment in the world. Furthermore, the mastery of walking is a family event which evokes affect laden parental responses. Parental attitudes color the emotional atmosphere in which the child learns to separate, physically, just as they influence the adolescent's reorganization of object ties. Depending upon their meaning for the parents, the child's increasingly autonomous excursions can bring either joy in achievement, or fear and anger. During adolescence, movement continues to reflect unconscious separation fears and conflicts about loss of the self and the internal object.

Children's ability to walk gives rise to realistic self-esteem and pleasure in competence. Erikson (1978) noted that the older child's sense of personal identity involves some awareness of the ego's functions and capabilities. Locomotion develops in the course of a period which is greatly colored by the acquisition of language, and by the growing capacity for attributing meaning to experience (Sullivan, 1953). Reality testing increases simultaneously with the understanding of symbols and the ability to communicate logically. Furthermore, language development adds to the complexity of self-esteem development and to the cognitive changes which occur in harmony with walking.

Locomotion and Acting Out

Antisocial and habitually acting out adolescents share a number of ego deficits of early origin. Fenichel (1945) described chronically acting-out adolescents as impulsive people who depend upon the external world to counteract narcissistic instabilities. Fenichel theorized that they suffered from an idealization of action and an inability to tolerate anxiety which contributed to a misalliance between the ego and the id. A weakness in symbolic functioning was said to predispose very impulsive youths to act out the unconscious residue of childhood trauma. Action therefore remained the primary means for reducing tension. Greenacre (1950) reported two related characteristics of the acting-out individual, a persistent belief in the magical power of action, and distortion of the connections between action, speech and thought. Adolescents' need for action has also been described, in theory, as a reaction formation to regressive passivity. Passivity has been correlated with adolescents' increased sexual drive, subsequent to puberty (Blos, 1962, 1979). Antisocial adolescents often lack planning skills and problem-solving abilities. Their cognitive capacities may be insufficiently developed to compensate for deficiencies in impulse control and frustration tolerance. Healthy adolescents consistently act in order to deflect anxiety, but impulsive, disturbed adolescents cling to the defensive need to act out. In Freud's theoretical framework, such characterological tendencies added to the compulsion to repeat in order to avoid infantile anxieties and repressed trauma.

During the course of lengthy analytic work, a young professional woman recalled with embarrassment that many of her adolescent shopping trips had involved compulsive shoplifting. She had been driven to steal clothing and jewelry from department stores, and these stolen articles had seemed to serve as magical amulets that insured her self continuity. Rather than experiencing pleasure in the possession of these articles, she had felt that she needed them at moments when her feelings and perceptions fused in a mass of unreality. In an early session, the patient remembered a recurrent dream.

She had been recuperating from life-threatening surgery in the dream as she was lying in a hospital recovery-room bed. The other patients and the hospital staff faded into the background, as the room became a theater, and then an amphitheater with thousands of spectators watching her. The dimensions of the recovery room kept expanding in size until, in a terrifying instant, it exploded into the horizon.

The symbolism of the principal feeling in the dream was bluntly clear. The patient and I both felt that the dream represented her feelings of disorientation and identity fragmentation. Although there was much that could have been said about the transference implications of the dream, I first asked the patient for her associations to the harrowing explosion, and to her fear and need for the audience. Her associations suggested that her wish to be rescued and to exhibit her most private feelings conflicted with an image of me as an annihilating, detached voyeur, who would be unreliable and unavailable to protect her from panic and persecutory scorn. My confusion and sense of fragmentation with this patient came into focus when I realized that she had been experiencing me as being like *thousands of spectators.* We subsequently uncovered her core experience of perceptual uncertainty, self-discontinuity, depersonalization and rage which, at times, had culminated in dystonic, antisocial actions. This woman's acting out defended her against identity loss. Later in the same session, she associated her history of shoplifting with an earlier childhood pattern of stealing. Her need for the admiration of an audience, in the dream, was also connected with her late adolescent compulsive pursuit of sexual partners whom she used to provide her with self-definition. For the first time, in the analysis, she began to connect momentary lapses in her sense of identity with a fear of feeling vulnerable and mistrustful.

A number of authors have highlighted object relations impairments in such patients with identity disturbance and antisocial traits. Winnicott (1956) maintained that the adolescent's degree of ego maturity in the face of environmental failures determined whether antisocial actions or psychotic breakdowns would occur. The habit of treating others exploitively was explored by Winnicott in clinical accounts of antisocial youths' assaultive demands on the environment to satisfy developmental needs which originated in the inner object world. Anna Freud (1949) found worthy of attention adolescents' fantasies of sadistic acting out, which derived from a combination of aggressive energies and inhibited phallic masturbation. This fusion of erotic and aggressive impulses played a significant part in her reports of the dynamics of antisocial behavior, as did the defensive retreat from the fear of dependency feelings and emotional surrender (A. Freud, 1952). Masterson likewise (1972) discussed borderline and narcissistic adolescents' structural deficits in terms of regressive part-self object units which were expressed in acting out. The frenzied pursuit of sexual activity, in perversions, has also been shown to be a form of acting out which offers relief from archaic identifications and internalized object relations (Khan, 1979). Susceptibility to depressive episodes and angry outbursts, in response to minor frustrations, adds to the reliance on acting out in adolescents whom Fenichel (1945) portrayed as instinct ridden. Disturbed, conduct disordered adolescents, like those with antisocial character trends, use acting out, and locomotion fantasies, in combating dysphoric, anxiety ridden states of identity loss.

Clinical Data

I will present two additional clinical vignettes which are aimed to convey the importance of acting out and locomotion themes in adolescents' identity loss. This encapsulated presentation will contrast a relatively healthy adolescent's use of locomotion fantasies with a very disturbed, borderline, antisocial adolescent's efforts to wrench needed satisfaction from external displacements of internal objects (Winnicott, 1956). This second, more disturbed, patient used acting out and movement fantasies in order to diminish death anxiety and marked identity loss. Both patients were compelled to effect a synthesis of action and movement fantasies in the course of their adolescent development.

> During the middle stage of therapy, a relatively healthy fourteen year old boy mentioned to me, in absolute seriousness, that he had fallen in love with a motorcycle. A sixteen year old boy, who had a history of antisocial behavior and gratuitous violence, reported that he had cut his wrists, deeply, immediately after learning that his girlfriend had destroyed her copy of his photograph.

The first patient's rapture over his motorcycle represented a complex important to note that a number of psychoanalytic theorists, of different orientations, have objected to Erikson's equation of maturity with identity formation. Guntrip and Kohut, for example, both rejected the concept of identity, as an idea which grasped only the surface of the personality, in favor of their own concepts of the self. The similarity between Mahler's description of toddlers' autonomous practicing, and Erikson's (1968) portrait of adolescents' role experimentation in the psychosocial moratorium has been examined by Brandt (1977). The adolescent process of inclusion of new phenomena into the self has been discussed, from a Freudian perspective, under the headings of character consolidation and separation-individuation, by Blos (1967), Fenichel (1959), Mahler (1975), and Pine (1982).

In summary, young children use movement play and fantasies to express their anxiety about psychic separateness and interpersonal separations. Adolescents continue to rebel against, and to seek out, unconscious union between the self and the object through action. Action is often employed by the adolescent both to further differentiation and to express unconscious conflicts with internalized objects. Habitually acting-out adolescents, who are prone to identity loss, remain limited in achieving integration and tolerating frustration. Psychoanalytic work with antisocial adolescents inevitably emphasizes the relationship between developmental conflicts, the family, and identity consolidation.

CHAPTER TEN

Narcissistic Adolescents

..... I threw a plate into the street, and was overjoyed to see it go to bits so merrily.... My neighbors continued to signify their approval and I was delighted to have amused them....

Sigmund Freud, quoting Goethe

The ubiquitous desire for attention readily finds its way into becoming a mainstay of the narcissistic adolescent's character organization. Out of the richness of narcissistic phenomena, the youth with this type of character trend, broadens the recurring wish for admiration into a dominant, fixed defensive process. This chapter will examine narcissistic adolescents' compulsive quest for admiration and merger which is driven by their need to ward off primitive fears of dependency and annihilation. My main objective will be to describe narcissistic adolescents' efforts to compel the analyst into a transference object relationship in which the patient fears and seeks being held in awe. Another primary aim will be to contrast Freudian, British object relations and interpersonal views of narcissistic youths' intransigent self-involvement and their dread of their internalized attachments. The approach I have chosen to this subject will entail a case presentation which will be used to illustrate these patients' object relations and character traits. As a part of this exploration, I will also emphasize that family processes strengthen the narcissistic adolescent's compensatory reliance on admiration and grandiosity. In the latter part of this final chapter, I will briefly refer to Masud Khan's ideas about narcissistic affects and to Harry Stack Sullivan's concept of participant observation, as the basis for a therapeutic approach with narcissistic adolescent patients. Analytic work with narcissistic adolescents requires an active, although not exclusively interpretative, engagement which focuses on the clinical inquiry and the therapeutic interaction.

Introduction

The Freudian, interpersonal and object relations theories of metapsychology have concentrated on different concepts to account for narcissistic adolescents' need for fusion with an admiring object. Theorists from each psychoanalytic orientation have noted these patients' insouciant self-centeredness, their projection of their demandingness, and their mercurial anger at their admirers' unavailability. For the extremely narcissistic youth, exploitative contact with an admirer becomes a driven compulsion which masks deflated grandiosity and low self-esteem. When the absence of an admirer is most deeply felt by adolescents with severe narcissistic trends, denied feelings of worthlessness and emptiness bring forth their underlying melancholic anxieties. For these adolescents, the feeling of being momentarily recognized and admired assuages their brittle self-esteem which has been eroded by family psychopathology. Such narcissistic preoccupations have been categorized as: the result of the adolescent's libidinal fixation with the body (Freud, 1914), extreme orality and a pathological self structure (Kernberg, 1975), the outcome of efforts to preserve the grandiose self (Kohut, 1971), and the manifestations of a narcissistic, phallic exhibitionism (Reich, 1933).

By way of introduction to this topic, I will first present two cursory examples of dreams in which the manifest content highlights the sustained urgency of narcissistic adolescents' need to counteract loneliness and emptiness by getting others to admire their self image. Analytic scrutiny brings to light both the characterological complexity, and the family dynamics of neurotic and more pathological adolescent narcissism.

An eighteen year old adolescent boy, who experienced frequent episodes of depression and severe temper outbursts, reported a dream in his second session. In the dream, this patient was driving a car recklessly along a winding mountain road with a close male friend as a passenger. He felt unconcerned about speeding, until the car crashed suddenly, and both he and his friend were killed in a terrible moment in the dream. According to the patient, the principal feeling in the dream was a powerful sense of excitement. His associations to the dream pointed to the pleasure of being treated reverentially, and to the mixture of danger and sexual excitement inherent in his getting high. When asked for his thoughts about his indifference to the car's speed, he noted that his mind often got lost in capturing his friends' attention. Additional associations suggested the rapidity with which he formed pseudoidentities, in order to remain the focus of others' admiration. The dream's manifest content, by itself, hinted at this young man's counterdepressive superiority, his expectation of immunity from danger and his omnipotent air of invincibility when he became the object of attention and devotion.

The symbolism of the speeding car referred, in part, to the manic quality of this patient's thrill seeking and phallic fantasies. Even without any exploration of its implications for the analytic relationship, the dream's terse symbolism suggested his self-destructive impulsivity, and the acuteness of his anxiety, when he was poorly defend against his loneliness and emptiness. The dream's manifest content, by itself, hinted at this young man's counterdepressive superiority. His expectation of being exempt from danger meshed with his omnipotent air of invincibility when he became the object of attention and devotion.

A sixteen year old girl, whose insecurity took the form of contemptuous arrogance with her family and friends, told me of a dream in which she went on a trip with her parents to a beach on the French Riviera. At a point in the dream when she was enjoying the admiring glances, which her body and her bathingsuit generated, she asked her mother for $5,000 spending money for the next weekend. Her mother gratified this request, and the patient reported that the immediate feeling in the dream was one of triumph. This patient's repressed shame, and her pervasive need for admiration and special treatment was profound. With only the slightest disguise, the dream recounted her unrecognized centering of her self-deprecation and shame on body experience, together with the family encouragement of her exploitativeness and sense of entitlement.

Both patients displayed a sorrowful degree of grandiosity, and a need for unstinting adoration, which pervaded all of their relationships, especially those which offered the prospect of merger. The lengths, to which these patients were compelled to go in order to sustain attention and admiration from their friends, reinforced the impression of their desperation and early deprivation. A number of my adolescent patients who have demonstrated a narcissistic character organization have exhibited this chilling reliance on others in order to maintain their own tenuous reality testing and self-esteem. They have been subject to elusive states of fusion, in which the manic excitement of feeling admired evaded depression and self-devaluation.

The parents of the type of adolescent I'm describing behave as though their teenager's individuation represents a narcissistic insult. The internalization of humiliation and disdainful family interactions deepens the narcissistic adolescent's defensive reliance on grandiosity and entitlement. Due to both their family's rejections, and their own fragile self-esteem, these adolescents' needs for recognition and attention are gradually transformed into an all-consuming preoccupation with admiration. As these adolescents remain entangled in the pathological family process, they grow more dependent on friends and romantic partners to satisfy their need to be recognized, and held in awe. The parents of adolescents, who have narcissistic character disorders, have been found to exhibit failures in self-esteem regulation, to expect perfection, and to use their adolescents to preserve their own psychic structure (Berkowitz, et al. 1974). By their incessant need to be the center of attention, such parents unwittingly tip the scale of the adolescent's narcissistic balance in favor of a falsely inflated self image which is incompatible with realistic aspirations (Blos, 1979; Egan & Kernberg, 1984). Kohut's (1971, 1977) work schematized narcissistic parents' inability to facilitate idealizations, and their reluctance to permit any discovery of their own shortcomings. Narcissistic adolescents' character consolidation occurs against the background of this type of family pathology.

Freudian Views of Narcissistic Character Trends

Freud's luminous work first recorded narcissistic adolescents' primary reliance on admiration to fuel their defensive self-aggrandizement. In Freud's (1914) essay on narcissism, he wrote that people with this type of personality were characterized by a self-infatuation which supported the withdrawal of libido from external objects. He conceived of their consequent erotic fixation, and their character pathology, as rendering them unsuitable for analytic treatment. Freud posited a stage of primary narcissism before the establishment of object relations. In his view, normal adolescent narcissism represented a stage of increased autoerotism and a decathexis of the infantile love objects. Extreme, or pathological, narcissism was incompatible with mature object relations. The ego ideal became the adolescent's replacement for the shattered illusion of omnipotence and the lost narcissism of childhood. Mature erotic love erased the vestiges of adolescent narcissistic attachments by transferring narcissism onto the object. In contemporary Freudian theory, pathogenic elements of Oedipal and preOedipal conflict are said to be reactivated by the demands of late adolescence. Furthermore, the character changes of late adolescence have been depicted as taking form with the final alliance of the id, ego, and superego, in which the Oedipus complex is resolved. With the final structuring of the personality during late adolescence, passive, dependent demands on the object are revived. During this period of heightened adolescent narcissism, Oedipal strivings may serve as a defense against narcissistic injuries (Grunberger, 1971). In his amplification of Freudian libido theory, Erikson (1956) noted that middle and late adolescents' self-esteem maintenance was part of the process of the formation of the ego identity. The intense wish to be the constant center of attention was determined, by Erikson, to be an example of regression in the service of "as if" identities. In addition to Erikson, several other Freudian ego psychologists have thematicly paired the characterological outcome of late adolescence with self-esteem disturbances.

Hartmann's (1958) concept of the neutralization of sexual and aggressive drives contained a view of narcissistic development which extended Freud's theory. According to Hartmann (1953), narcissistic character trends resulted from a cathexis of self representations in which there was a greater libidinal investment of self images. Heightened narcissism amounted to a libidinal cathexis of the self. Although Hartmann's reworking of structural theory did not emphasize narcissism in adolescence, Jacobson did stress adolescents' shifts in narcissism as a result of their adjustments to castration anxiety. Jacobson (1964) assigned both defensive functioning in the face of trauma, and self-esteem maintenance, to the superego. Her work on early idealization and the ego ideal predated Kohut's ideas about the existence of an independent line of narcissistic development. Blos (1979) argued that, for males, narcissistic character disorders were best understood as a pathology of prolonged adolescent overvaluation of the mind and the body. His theoretical position has come the closest to an object relations perspective. Yet, in the aftermath of Erikson's, Hartmann's and Jacobson's modifications of Freudian drive theory, threats to adolescents' self-esteem have been understood more in terms of structural problems and instinctual danger than in terms of either internalized object relations or family processes. Additional Freudian investigations of narcissistic adolescents' intrapsychic conflicts have been provided by Bleiberg (1987), Chavis (1990), Settlage (1977), and Spruiell (1975).

Relational and Interpersonal Theories of Narcissistic Character Trends

From Klein and Fairbairn's point of view, narcissistic adolescents were unduly embroiled in struggles with both depressive anxiety and schizoid-paranoid dynamics. In Kleinian theory, pathological narcissism reflected a retreat from inner annihilation and the envious spoiling of the breast. Prior to Klein's work, Freud's ideas about intense feelings of envy had led to his hypothesis that envy was dynamicly interwoven with paranoia and conflicts about sexual object choice. W. Reich (1933) elaborated a classical Freudian approach to narcissistic character traits which had some bearing on contemporary views of internal object relationships in narcissistic character trends. Reich claimed that a narcissistic barrier, which was inherent in neurotic defenses, increased all resistances to the psychoanalytic process. He suggested that the analyst, as a transference figure, was always experienced as the enemy of patients' self-esteem.

This notion of a narcissistic component to resistance paralleled Sullivan's (1953, 1956) emphasis on failures in empathy, as the stimulus for both the developmental transmission of anxiety, and the destructive increase in patients' anxiety during psychotherapy. An active analytic presence, with adolescent patients, which included the importance of developing an inquiry, was implicit in Sullivan's model of participant observation. Interpersonal analysts have preferred this concept of participant observation to either the therapeutic alliance, or the working alliance (Chrzanowski, 1979; Hirsh and Aron, 1991). Narcissistic character traits were sketched, in Sullivan's systemic understanding of damaged self-esteem, as predominately preadolescent, egocentric expectations of unlimited service. Fromm-Reichmann's (1959) accounting of adolescents' loneliness provided another interpersonal explanation for their heightened narcissism.

Both Horney and Fromm linked narcissism to a sterile, neurotic character orientation which made little allowance for relatedness and productivity. Horney (1939, 1945) offered a thoughtful critique of Freud's theory of narcissism which was remarkably similar to Kohut's later views of narcissistic development. For Horney, (as well as Sullivan and Fromm), narcissism was a very salient feature of neurosis, in that, the neurotic child substituted admiration, and an inflated self-importance for love and emotional security. Fromm (1973) maintained that the narcissist combined the receptive character's longings for a magical incorporated object, with the marketing character's disregard for his, or her, inner qualities. According to both Fromm and Horney, relinquishing narcissism required the dissolution of incestuous childhood ties which provided security. The neurotic's identification with the dictatorial demands of an unrealistic, idealized self image accounted for narcissistic vulnerability to depression and volatile self-esteem.

Kohut (1971, 1972) believed that traumatic deflations of the young child's omnipotence and grandiosity resulted in fixations with the grandiose self and the idealized parental image. Such deprived adolescents were designated, by Kohut, as being "mirror hungry", because they craved during adolescence, the mirroring they missed in early childhood. Winnicott (1971) similarly viewed the child's damaged self-esteem as an outcome of developmental failures in the use of the mother's face, as a precursor of the mirror. Unlike Horney and Sullivan, Kohut postulated a vertical split in these adolescent's personalities, which explained their vacillation between grandiosity and diminished self-esteem. Kohut's outline of development departed from Freudian developmental theory, and his self psychology clinical theory differed from Freud's approach by its emphasis on analyzing resistances to the narcissistic transferences. A character organization, which is based on self-inflation, exhibitionism and exploitation has also been described, by neoFreudian, interpersonal theorists, as the outgrowth of excessive neurotic insecurity and dependency (Horney, 1950). In interpersonal theory, narcissism has been portrayed, not as a distinct character type, but as the core problem of damaged self-esteem in all neurotic character organization (Barnett, 1980B). The two patients I mentioned, and a third patient, whom I will discuss more fully, all displayed these characterological tendencies along with an intense dread of both early object relationships and adolescent mourning. To different degrees, they shared the neurotic or schizoid tendency to treat others as though they lacked intrinsic value.

Case Illustration

I will refer to a particular session which occurred during the beginning period of my work with a seventeen year old boy. The session exemplified typically adolescent issues in the midst of an emerging narcissistic character organization. It documented the patient's struggle with deficits in his body image, his underlying shame and his fragile sense of identity. My discussion of the session will stress that this boy's impelling need for admiration, and his incipient grandiosity were expressions of both his ongoing experience in the family, and his primitive anxieties in relation to internalized objects.

The patient, whom I will call Sam, displayed the consummate self-absorption, and several other characteristics of adolescents who have narcissistic character disorders, such as excessive variability in self-esteem, a confused self image, and a chronic need for admiration of physical and mental attributes. In spite of these traits, he did not cultivate either serious antisocial tendencies, or an imperious sense of entitlement and contempt for others. The tendency to demand special treatment was present in nascent form in Sam's interactions. Nevertheless, he had ethical values and ideals, and his relationships hinted at considerable empathy. Sam lacked the marked exploitativeness and insensitivity which are diagnostic indications of pathological narcissism in youngsters who demean other people by compelling them to serve as a gratifying audience.

Presenting Complaints

Sam asked to begin treatment in his third year of high school, because of his deteriorating relationship with his parents, and his use of alcohol. He was an intelligent, articulate boy whose reported inability to tolerate any criticism, and need for constant attention suggested narcissistic personality features. Sam told me in the first interview about his worry that his previously sporadic alcohol use was fast becoming a more frequent habit. Left to his own devices, Sam's social successes and academic achievements proved insufficient to protect him from depressive self- devaluation. Although adolescents commonly undergo fluctuations in self-esteem, Sam's self-esteem varied dramatically according to his friends' attentiveness.

When he was the center of attention at a party with his friends, Sam felt admired and inflated with a false sense of grandiosity. Nevertheless, he felt depleted when he compared himself with his friends, and depressed when they disappointed him. Sam's wish for attention from his mother, and his girlfriend, reached proportions which indicated an almost omnipotent need to control their availability. He was pressed to preserve the fleeting enjoyment of his friends' attention in ways which courted identity loss. In addition, Sam feared rejection because of his imperfections, and he became severely confused about his body image, but not to the point of losing reality testing. However, unlike adolescents with thoroughly narcissistic personalities, Sam's intermittent, exhibitionistic demands for attention were not accompanied by a grandiose lack of empathy.

History

My periodic meetings with Sam's parents elicited a great deal of data about the family's contributions to the evolution of Sam's character trends. Sam was the oldest of four siblings, and he had one younger sister and two younger brothers. Although I have chosen not to present the chronology of Sam's developmental history, it was noteworthy that both he and his younger sister had been separated from their parents for long periods of time when they were cared for by their grandparents. Sam was between five and seven years of age at the time of these separations. His parents' longstanding, volatile relationship was based on much mutual disappointment and covert hostility.

Sam's mother appeared to be a compassionate, seriously depressed, partially immobilized woman who lacked the energy to face either the frequent arguments between Sam and his father, or Sam's needs for emotional support. Sam's father was a sophisticated, highly narcissistic, thoroughly self-absorbed individual who evidenced delusional beliefs about his uniqueness and importance in the community. His chief mode of relating to his adolescent children had come to consist of bombastic lectures, interspersed with the sarcastic use of ridicule, whenever his perfectionistic standards were not met. The reports of the family interactions suggested themes of envy and Oedipal rivalry between Sam and his father. Sam's father seemed to initiate most of the competitions. Apparently, he felt envious of Sam's personality assets and Sam's previously positive relationship with his mother. Sam's neediness led to inconsiderate requests on his part, such as, frequent requests for advances of money, and his irritability aggravated the arguments with his father. Sam's father projected his own negative traits onto Sam, while retaliating against him by means of criticisms and humiliating jokes.

Sam was a highly productive, well organized person in spite of his affective lability and fragile self-esteem. He maintained an A average in high school, led an active social life, and worked at a part time job on weekends. His alienation from his mother had lasted for several years, but he was close to two of his siblings. Sam was overly sensitive to shifts in his friends' moods and availability. Too often, he exhausted himself, socially, due to his inability to retain the mental image and the feeling of his enjoyment of others' company. His sexual life reflected adolescent doubts about his sexual capability superimposed upon a strong need for symbiotic closeness with his female friends. Sam unconsciously viewed sexual contact through the prism of annihilation anxiety and the terror of an infantile reliance on his girlfriend. In spite of Sam's high intelligence and his capacity for self-reflection, he lacked insight into his degree of dependence and his counterphobic sexual longings. Although Sam could be gregarious and charming, his solitary depressive moods occasionally resonated with self-hatred, couched in suicidal ideation. Hysterical components were also apparent, such as, self-dramatization and the impulsive discharge of tension filled moments of an affective overload.

Clinical Material

During one particular session, this patient's depressive anxiety and manic posture emerged clearly in relation to his staggering need for attention and approval. If the dynamic themes of the session had been listed systematically, beginning with the surface content, they would have taken the form of the following outline.

1)   Defensive anger and excessive talking with avoidance of grief, rage, humiliation, and shame.
2)   A defective body image.
3)   Fear of being seen naked and of phallic strivings.
4)   Terror of disintegration and the loss of identity.

5)   Early longings for attention and nurturance.
6)   Need for (and fear of) girlfriend mother.
7)   Manic defense against the need for the alienated internal father.
8)   Incipient self acceptance and increased empathy.

Taken as a whole, the themes of the session pointed to the repressed anxiety, and the rich complexity of Sam's character traits, near the final stage of his adolescent development.

The excerpts from the session, which are listed below, detail Sam's experience with his girlfriend at a party, and they include several of my interventions. My interventions in the session alternated between listening, asking questions which helped Sam focus his feelings, and analyzing my reactions to his pleas for responsiveness. Sam's barrage of words reflected his need to impress and to be admired as a mechanism for maintaining emotional distance.

"As far as everything went, you know it was like, I thought I was pretty funny the whole night, in the beginning of the night. You know like I didn't feel any tension, and Liz and I were getting along great and everything. Then just some time along the night there were a couple of competitions. You know like she was still playing tough. I couldn't have her that way. Like she would act like she didn't care. And rather than me, almost like treating me a little like shit. Rather than me treating, you know like kissing up to her. I would kind of act the same way. So we kind of ignored each other. We play that game with each other, which kind of got out of hand. But there were things that got her made like, you know what I mean? Before, everything was great, everything was great. Like everyone knew me and I knew everybody. So she was impressed by that because everybody kept saying Hello. A girl came running up to me, gave me like two kisses on the cheek, you know, everybody was really in a happy mood.

The thing that kind of might have ruined it was when I went to the bathroom. You know I washed my hands, I took a piece of paper, I dropped the piece of paper, then when I went to pick it up I banged by head on the sink. And, I got a pretty big gash in my head. I mean I still have it. I don't know if you want to see it. But it's pretty big. It's like about 2,3 inches. And you know I needed stitches but when I hit my head I didn't think it was that bad. I didn't think it was that bad at all. I just thought it was, I mean I got the gash because I hit a sharp object. And you know, the first thing I said to myself is like I'm not going to let anything ruin...the night. And I was worried about my hair. Like I didn't care about the cut. I hung out for like 5-10 minutes and it stopped bleeding.

And then I just kind of looked at a friend who asked What's the matter?, What's the matter?, So I told him, but I whispered it. And then Liz was kind of curious about what's going on, so I told her anyway. ....And I was like, it didn't bother me at all, the cut. I handled it. And it wasn't that painful, I mean it hurt in a little way. She worried more about it than I did, so that was kind of getting me annoyed.

Like I said, it kind of threw everything off track. Kind of ruined it just a little bit. And you know she was worried and everybody else was kind of worried. I wasn't. I was the only person that really wasn't worried".

(Even though we could have pursued Sam's idealized self image, his distancing and his potential perception of me as being disinterested and neglectful, I asked him what was it about Liz's concern that got him annoyed?)

"She was too concerned. You know. Rather than having fun she was more concerned about my cut than me. You know I really didn't, I didn't want to deal with the cut until tomorrow. The least she could have done was not to have told me that I was just trying to be brave. I'm not trying to be brave, I just didn't want to think about it. I mean what are we doing to do? Go to the hospital and ruin the night? I mean the night's here we might as well not think about it until tomorrow".

(Later in the session I asked Sam to describe his feelings about himself, in relation to Liz).

"Well, I was disappointed for not getting the attention I wanted. Sometimes we talked about it...I'm aware that sometimes I want so much love because it's this emptiness. Because I was always ignored when I was little, as far as the love from my parents went. There's this emptiness inside me that no matter how much I'm going to love somebody, it almost seems that my love is never fulfilled. I have to realize that. But at the same time, I think that what's really going to help is that if I see Liz or whoever, I have to realize that when I hang out with...because I was reading something about the way lovers should be, and it should be being aware of each other's parts, but never holding them. Never giving it away to the other person. Being yourself first. Learning how to get along with the other person at the same time. In other words, never giving yourself away to the other person. Always holding yourself back...I kind of realize that. You know like me and Liz were getting really close after the party. I almost sensed that closeness. The first thing I said to myself is the fact that we had that experience brought us closer. It wasn't so much that we spent so much time together. It was an intense moment. Then I was saying to myself, maybe I don't need her that much. We had an argument that Saturday and she came over with a friend and I was ignoring her. I was drunk, you know I was drunk that whole weekend, and I felt bad about myself. Cause I worked out so hard, I felt like I looked so small. That's the other thing, that's a big part that bothered me this week.

I just feel that I'm a lot skinnier and smaller than people think I am, because I'm always wearing baggy clothes. I'm always trying to make myself look big. I'm afraid they're not going to get what they really want to expect. If I see somebody and they got a scar on their face, right away that to me says. You know it kind of turns me off a little bit when that person says, oooo, that's disgusting. And although, that person might be your friend, that scar has an effect on you, just a little bit. So I feel like if my arms are too skinny or my legs are too skinny and I feel like a wimp, it's going to deplete the relationship. They won't think of me as much. So it's like me losing the value of myself".

(After some additional material, Sam returned to his feelings about his body and his feelings about being seen undressed. By that point, it seemed that his need for admiration had fused with both his wish to satisfy me as his distracted mother, and his need for vigilance against his father's hostile intrusiveness.)

    "In my fantasies...I thought I was going to be the biggest guy on the beach. A hunk, every girl's dream. And between relationships I wanted to do that. I want to have this great body so the girls aren't disappointed. So like for myself I want to look great, but at the same time I don't want to disappoint them. I always feel like I'm a pleaser to the girls. Like if I have sexual intercourse with somebody, I feel like I have to please the girl first before I can please myself. I'm a satisfier, not a self satisfier. I'm afraid that she's not going to be satisfied with my body.

    There's a theory I've been thinking about the whole week. I'm saying to myself, two people think like me. And I've been having a hard time judging myself, looking in the mirror. Looking at my body and I'm not satisfied with it so nobody else can be satisfied with it. But I don't know, I'm saying two people think like me. Well I can look at my friend and think well, he's pretty big, look at him. Then I look at him and go, he's tiny. So people do have the judgement of a person, if he's small or not. That's what I'm afraid of".

(My response was to ask Sam for his thoughts about feeling small and weak. His acknowledgement that this feeling had been a highly defended aspect of his self image led to further depressive feelings.)

    "So I'm judging myself in a very negative way. I'm trying to figure out how that has an effect on people. I think it has a lot to do with the bad feelings that I have about myself. You know all the bad things I experienced. I feel like shit, like there is something wrong with me.

    This summer there's so much pressure on the way I look. Because we're spending so much time outside. You know right away there's an almost instant reminder, the fact that I look worse as soon as I get a little sun. It almost had an instant relationship to all the bad feelings I had with the beach. I remember one thing, I use to go there a lot. I used to try to sun bathe. And I'd look at myself and think... Oh, man my face looks so ugly. You know I hated that. And that brings back all the bad things, that fight I had with Liz. So the beach, or anything outside, sunbathing, whatever has me being disappointed in myself. Its' me being disappointed in myself.

It brings back all these memories. It brings back all these memories, and I'm also afraid of the memories it's going to create for people right now. Like as far as Liz and her being disappointed with the way I look.

There's a real loneliness about it. I don't want to socialize, I have a hard time...I drank Friday. It has an effect on me the next day because I drank. So then, I feel like if I drank the next day, I really don't have that much to say. I'm isolated and everything in my head is blocked. So, I figured I'd get back into it just by drinking".

(At that point there was silence. After several shifts in his associations and changes of the subject, Sam later spoke of his slightly improved relationship with his mother.)

As the treatment progressed beyond this session, Sam increasingly felt the impact of his unconscious dialogue with preoccupied admirers who failed to treat him as an object of devotion. My discussion of this session will stress Sam's wish for admiration in the transference, and it will offer Freudian, interpersonal and object relations approaches to organizing the clinical material. Each model has much to offer our understanding of this kind of patient's emotional life.

Discussion

Early in the above session, my questions underscored Sam's defensive anger, and his lack of insight into his persecutory affects and arrogant demandingness. My more directive questions linked his alcohol use with his vulnerability to lapses in self- esteem, and his panic about identity loss. Although Sam had initially made little assessment of either his drinking, or his flight from depression, he came to connect his alcohol use with his anger, and his anxiety about feeling flawed and unlovable. Even though my questions did not directly challenge Sam's talking, as a resistance, they aimed to help him experience his affective states and to trace the unconscious motives for his defensive strategies.

Several times in the session, Sam referred to a minor physical injury as a metaphor for psychic injury, somatic preoccupations, and anxiety about disintegration. By his own account, Sam's body image had become a depository for feelings of worthlessness and compensatory grandiosity. Sam's vacillating feelings about his body, which were poured out in other sessions, evoked memories of feelings of envy, and disruptions of admiration for his body self. He eventually recognized a fear of being seen naked which surpassed castration anxiety. This fear combined an early, anxiety filled wish for parental admiration of his body and developmental interferences with body image consolidation (Greenacre, 1958). Sam's poorly articulated fantasy about suicide conveyed his hatred of his own neediness as well as his frustration at his failure to excite attention and admiration. His complaints about his girlfriend broached his feelings of deprivation and betrayal, as well as his perception of himself as a victimized hero. Sam's Oedipal feelings were not always well organized, but his relationships with females were largely governed by the expectation of humiliation. Although I did not interpret it at the time, it seemed that Sam utilized the session to express his internalized anger and his transferential wish to feel deeply acknowledged. Such wishes were threatening, not only because of the late adolescent's defenses against dependency needs and desires for nurturance, but also because of their evocation of homosexual anxieties in relation to the negative Oedipal father. Sam's statements about his disappointment in his girlfriend contained a transference reference to the limitations of my ability to admire him, and to protect him from instances of inner disorganization. Many of Sam's interactions with his friends, and much of the unconscious communication in the sessions, expressed the hurt and rage of this renewed search for a failed inner relationship.

In a study of the family experience of suicidal adolescents with narcissistic character features, Shapiro and Freedman (1985) reported similar characterological problems and family dynamic issues. Insufficient maternal involvement with their infantile bodies led, during latency, to these youngsters' feelings of hopelessness and fantasies of self-sufficiency. Following the stresses and dependency conflicts of puberty, their envy of others, and hatred at never having been special, came closer to consciousness. My principal contention about narcissistic adolescents' families has been that parental narcissism perpetuates projective processes which express devaluation and humiliation. Feelings of rage, shame and emptiness are strikingly significant in their reactivation of these adolescent's dissociated anxieties. Such feelings evoke the desperation of early abandonments which shapes suicidal despair. Ongoing family interactions reinforce, throughout adolescence, narcissistic defenses against the damaged self-esteem and the primitive anxieties which underlie the emergent character organization.

Transference - Countertransference

At the onset of Sam's treatment, I had indicated that it was necessary for him to experience the mourning, and depressive moods, which were implicit in his feelings of emptiness. Sam's outbursts of temper and demandingness were typically externalized and projected. Yet, Sam tried to merge with others when they provided him with consistent approval and admiration. Prior to the above session, Sam's rage at his mother had gradually come to light as a much earlier issue than his resentment of his father's bullying. Sam's transferential desperation stemmed from an unsatisfied pre-Oedipal need to be fully recognized and defined by his parents' responses. Freud first described such a fixation as a narcissistic enslavement to the object which could be projected onto an audience.

At the beginning of our work, Sam's dread of dependency and humiliation had been displaced onto a fear of what he perceived to be my power over him. Sam felt terrified that I would either humiliate and destroy him, or surreptitiously force him to dismiss his feelings of anger and his perceptions of his family. On the surface, his fear of my illusory power filled him with a foreboding which masked his terror of helplessness and dependency. The wish for admiration and fusion beneath this fear was repeatedly played out in Sam's relationships, as well as in the transference-countertransference exchanges. Sam gradually became aware of the extent of his self-devaluation and self-contempt, as I alternately became his preoccupied mother, and his demanding father in the transference. Sam's dissociated wishes for attention and admiration acquired more specific meanings, as they occurred in our interaction. His inevitable disappointments in me enriched his capacity to tolerate disappointments in himself, and other without devaluation, and shame or the need for constant admiration.

At a point in one of the following sessions, I asked Sam to consider if his hatred of his mother might have been the result of both his unacknowledged dependency needs, and his fear that he could be invaded and robbed of his perceptions. I had wondered earlier whether the young child Sam might have merged with his mother out of disappointment, as well as fear of his own Oedipal hatred and his aversion to his father. In spite of his dependency leanings and his search for comfort and admiration, Sam's greatest fear was of an utter dependency on a lethal, intrusive, internalized parent, who would be unresponsive, and unavailable to him as an auxiliary ego.

One aspect of my countertransference was initially surprising. At first, it was puzzling that I was envious of Sam's charm and the reported glory of his social successes. It was unsettling for me to realize that I felt competitive with Sam for the attentions of his female admirers. Sam's envy interfered with the duration and the intensity of his attachments. His apparent fear of my envy and competitiveness contributed to his uncertainty about my capacity to withstand his mistrust without deliberate retaliations. He both envied and felt relieved by my efforts, and by his girlfriend's attempts, to resist his demands for a perfect attentiveness. From an object relations perspective, my envy and jealousy of Sam made sense as an expression of my depressive response to his depressive position and his paranoid-schizoid conflicts. On an interpersonal level, Sam initially retreated from emotional contact with me in his pursuit of perfection, but not to the extent of the unmitigated narcissist. My competitive feelings reflected an originally unrecognized identification with Sam's father's hostility and his hyperbolic role in the family transactions. Sam's difficulty in admiring either his father, or me added to his problems with integrating stable, positive self images. Denigrations and competitive taunts were frequently used by Sam's father, as weapons, to subvert Sam's efforts to individuate and to negotiate a *detente* with his mother. Sam had memories of being enticed by his father into a mutual admiration which was abruptly and unpredictably replaced by commonplace humiliations. Sam's need to excite admiration, and the transference-countertransference exchanges of envy in the sessions, both illustrated Sullivan's view of participant observation as continuous processes of mutual influence. These exacerbations of envy likewise suggested Klein's hypothesis about the dynamic tie of envy to primitive anxiety during the paranoid-schizoid position.

As I have already noted, Sam's character traits slanted his misperceptions of interpersonal interactions, as much as they organized his sexual and aggressive conflicts. His narcissistic features also consisted of well practiced, unconscious responses to the destructiveness of the past, and present family psychopathology. His character trends were simultaneously comprised of characteristic defensive maneuvers against the dreaded experience of annihilation, abandonment, and humiliation.

Case Summary

By the time of the above session, Sam's depressive tendencies and self-esteem problems had come to acquire the beginning status of narcissistic character traits. These traits reflected the underlying affective states and longstanding relational configurations I have described. Thus, Sam's demandingness, his hypersensitivity, and his lapses in self-esteem all reiterated the legacy of both his internal object ties and the continuing family process. Sam's episodic bouts of drinking were dynamicly related to his defensive denial of mourning and his depressive moods. They kept at bay his painful feelings of loss, and his disappointment in himself, whenever he began to feel the effects of an admirer's absence. Sam struggled to overcome his identifications with his mother's self-devaluation and his father's humiliating attacks. Nevertheless, the strength of Sam's identifications with his father's bluster, and his mother's hopelessness, added to his frenetic retreat from the fear of humiliation and dependency. His incipient grandiosity similarly defended him against the threat of being humiliated and annihilated.

Because of Sam's hysterical components, he vacillated, during dysphoric moods, between private states of dispassionate gloom and public displays of self-dramatization. Sam's developing sense of entitlement stemmed from multidetermined feelings of inadequacy, which were frequently reinforced by his father's disapproval and his mother's unresponsiveness. As a result of Sam's desperate longings for attention, and his impulsivity, his behavior elicited responses from people which were akin to his mother's withdrawal and his father's hostile intrusiveness. All of these difficulties galvanized the ferocious intensity of Sam's need for attention. His transactions with the interpersonal world, and the world of inner objects, were mediated by a narcissistic, albeit, hysterical, character organization.

Sam's rudimentary progress in treatment was suggested, during the above session, by his spontaneously identifying his depressive moods and his exhibitionistic tendencies with memories of feeling isolated and abandoned in the family. Sam began to internalize the analytic process of empathic inquiry, and to find his petulant exhibitions of narcissistic pique increasingly dystonic. Near the end of the above session, Sam started to discuss ephemeral periods of calm which had previously eluded him. During moments in subsequent sessions when I felt less competitive, Sam began to allow himself to feel dependent and to experience the nucleus of a peaceful self- containment. He eventually began to tolerate silence and feelings of loneliness in the transference. In keeping with instances of his newfound inner harmony during a phase of treatment which lasted about two years, Sam experienced less reactivity, and less manic pressure to be constantly engaging. As Sam achieved greater self-other differentiation, there was less of an addiction to the pursuit of admiration and greater mutuality in his relationships. Sam succeeded with aplomb in using the therapeutic process to deal with his underlying depressive trends, and to achieve a more clearly defined identity and self representations. This concise case presentation has drawn attention to characterological factors which contributed to a protean narcissistic vulnerability.

Further Relevant Literature

Freud first singled out both the attention seeking aspects of childrens' drives and the instability of the narcissist's grandiose fantasies. On the basis of Anna Freud's work with defensive processes, the importance of the narcissist's identification with the humilator has been emphasized as a characterological defense against the fear of humiliation (Adler, 1986; Rothstein, 1984).From a Freudian perspective, Settlage (1977) also documented narcissistic adolescents' transference manifestations of abandonment anxiety and plummeting self-esteem, which, he felt, were the aftereffects of an infantile rapproachment crisis. My overall understanding of treatment issues with narcissistic adolescents has been enhanced by the Freudian, interpersonal and object relations clinical models, including Horney's and Kohut's formulations about self-idealization and self-abnegation. My close monitoring of Sam's self-esteem reiterated elements of technique which resembled both the self psychology, and the interpersonal clinical model. However, the analytic work with this patient was most informed by Sullivan's concept of participant observation, and by Khan's ideas about patients' symbiotic enticement of the analyst in the transference.

In a study of narcissistic adolescents' transference patterns, Tylim (1978) emphasized the importance of one of Kohut's chief ideas. Tylim supported Kohut's belief that the cathexis of either the grandiose self, or the idealized parental image, curtailed narcissistic patients' degree of fragmentation. In Kohut's discussion of his theory's allegiance to classical Freudian metapsychology, he advocated reliance on interpretative reconstruction of empathic failures in the transference (Goldberg, 1985). However, in contrast to the interpersonal treatment model, Kohut cautioned against the use of questions as a technique which was inconsistent with analytic work in the empathic mode (Miller, 1985).

Klein's (1935) formative influence, on both Winnicott's and Khan's ideas about self-esteem, was keenly present in her account of the role of the manic defense in controlling internal objects. In an enlargement of Klein's views, in an entirely new direction, Winnicott's descriptions of self-esteem disturbances considered early failures in the use of the mother as a mirror of the self. Like Sullivan and Klein, Winnicott (1956) used the term, primitive anxiety, to refer to profound threats to ego integrity resulting from, what he termed, "infantile responses to impingement". Based on Winnicott's contributions, Khan depicted the compelling affectivity of narcissistic adolescents and young adults who revealed symbiotic relatedness. Early overindulgence, followed by deprivation, in his view, led such adolescents to failures in modulating aggression and in separation-individuation. Khan (1972) later revised his position with the realization that the narcissist's symbiotic relatedness constitutes a defense against regression to an infantile "resourceless dependency". In a subsequent paper, Khan (1989) described the dynamics of a twenty-two year old "as if" youth, who, like Sam, employed his aggression in order to strengthen his narcissistic ideal of perfection. Ameliorative states of regression and dependency have been discussed extensively by Balint (1968) and Bion (1967), as well as by Fairbairn, Khan, and Winnicott.

One might ask if a clinical inquiry, which is central to the interpersonal treatment model, interferes with the narcissistic adolescent's ability to idealize, or to feel catastrophic threats and to breakdown in the transference. On the contrary, it seems that the analyst's responses and failures allow the patient to develop sufficient trust to relive the dangers of dependency and annihilation. It has been my impression, that by the willingness to ask questions, as well as to interpret, analysts allow adolescent patients to come to grips with the enactments of their dependency needs, and deficits, as well as their dreaded internalized object relations. The establishment of a clinical inquiry redresses narcissistic adolescents' self-deceptions and their compelling needs for vigilant attention, both inside and outside of the transference. In the spirit of Sullivan and Horney, Bromberg (1983) described the confirmed narcissist as being wedged "between the mirror and the mask" of ingenuous performances which are designed to preserve the supremecy of the grandiose self. Contemporary neoFreudian theorists, in general, have delineated the defensive processes, and the flawed transactions, by which the narcissistic personality maintains the illusion of perfect self-sufficiency.

Summary

According to Ovid's version of the Narcissus myth, Narcissus killed himself out of despair that his reflected self image turned out to be an illusion. Adolescents with narcissistic character traits suffer from acute sensitivities to rejection along with an almost omnipotent need to control others' availability. Narcissistic adolescents' efforts to preserve the fragile feeling of being acknowledged give way to an habitual need for admiration.   Family transactions involving fears of annihilation and humiliation augment these adolescents' wishes to become the continuous object of admiration and devotion. In its less extreme form, their longing to be recognized and validated can be understood as a universal occurrence.   In its ultimate manifestations, their need to be admired reflects both a pathological dependency and a breakdown in the differentiation of self and object images.   For the less disturbed adolescent, with narcissistic features, the admirer is used to obtain approval and the validation of acceptability. The severely disturbed narcissistic adolescent utilizes the admirer to solidify the sense of identity, to maintain grandiosity, and to ward off threats to body and ego integrity. The exceedingly great degree of the highly narcissistic youth's need for admiration dooms the object to fail in transforming the self. During analytic treatment, adolescents with narcissistic character disturbance reveal both family, and intrapsychic aspects of their underlying addiction to feeling admired. Addictive proclivities defend them against a depressive core of poorly differentiated states and preverbal, primitive anxieties which their families help perpetuate.

Epilogue

Goethe's early memory of his histrionic display captured the symbolism of the narcissistic youth's need for the perfect audience to sustain self-esteem. According to Freud, morbid adolescent self-preoccupation resulted from a pathology of narcissism in which libido remained within the self. In interpersonal theory, narcissism was said to emerge in different neurotic forms in relationship to the dominant character trend, but narcissistic phenomena always occurred in proportion to the damage to the self. For Klein, and her followers, the need for self and object images of perfection originated in infantile anxiety about disintegration. The yearnings of the depressed ego arose from the fantasy of having smashed the object into bits, and from a sense of futility about is reconstruction. As a consequence of Freud's clinical papers and his paper on narcissism, his expanded discussion of character trends foreshadowed the partial convergence of the psychoanalytic clinical theories of adolescents' character analysis.

By way of conclusion, I would like to refer to a final example - my work with an unrelated, brilliant, marginally functioning student in her early twenties whose borderline character features reinforced an affecting core of primitive anxiety.

This woman came to be comfortably tolerant of her belief that she had the ability to control terrorist attacks by receiving messages from flocks of pigeons which flew over buildings in a specific New York City neighborhood. Her complacent belief in this special power offered palliative relief from the entrenched experience of feeling mercilessly scrutinized, and ruthlessly controlled, by introjected figures who stimulated uncompromising fear and hate. Also evident in relation to this patient's exalted sense of specialness, were dissociated feelings of emptiness and rigorous fears of disintegration.

Like many of the other patients I have described, this woman's adolescence had been a critical period for the erosion of her reality testing and the consolidation of her character pathology. After considerable effort to retain her defensive grandiosity during therapy, she eventually she sought to transform into an integrated whole, the composite of her identity fragments and her areas of healthy functioning. The current psychoanalytic theories of adolescence consist of keenly observed views about not only the obstacles to the late adolescent's maturation, but also the dread of disorganization and death which underlies psychopathology.

The final chapters of this volume have highlighted primitive anxiety states in adolescents' character disturbance. I have tried to demonstrate that, for each psychoanalytic orientation, the resolution of anxieties about annihilation of the self and the object facilitates characterological change. The passage of time has not diminished the value of either Freud's theory of adolescence, or the importance, for clinical work, of Sullivan's portrait of the adolescent developmental process with its affinity for the "dread, horror and loathing" of dissociated experience. The psychoanalytic metapsychological theories have supplemented each other in their elucidation of adolescence as the developmental period which consolidates the enduring pattern of the inner characteristics of the person.

REFERENCES

Abraham, K. (1924), The influence of oral eroticism in character formation. In: *The Selected Papers of Karl Abraham*. London: Hogarth Press, 1966.

Abraham, K. (1925), Character formation on the genital level of libido. In: *Selected Papers on Psychoanalysis*. London: Hogarth Press.

Adler, G. (1986), Psychotherapy of the narcissistic personality disorder patient: Two contrasting approaches. *American Journal of Psychiatry*, 143, 430-436.

Aichhorn, A. (1935), *Wayward Youth*. New York: Viking Press.

Aichhorn, A. (1964), The narcissistic transference of the juvenile imposter. In: O. Fleischmann, P. Kramer, & H. Ross, (Eds.) *Delinquency and Child Guidance: Selected Papers by August Aichhorn*. New York: International Universities Press.

Alexander, F. (1933), The relation of structural and instinctual conflicts. *Psychoanalytic Quarterly*, 2, 181-207.

Arieti, S. (1974), *Interpretation of Schizophrenia*. New York: Basic Books.

Bach, S. and Schwartz, L. (1972), A dream of Marquis de Sade. *Journal of the American Psychoanalytic Association*, 20,451-474.

Balint, M. (1968), *The Basic Fault: Therapeutic Aspects of Regression*. London: Tavistock Publications.

Bandura, W. (1959), *Adolescent Aggression, A Study of the Influence of Child Training, Practice and Family Relationships*. New York: Ronald Press.

Barnett, J. (1978), Insight and therapeutic change. *Contemporary Psychoanalysis*, 14, 534-544.

Barnett, J. (1980A), Interpersonal processes, cognition, and the analysis of character. *Contemporary Psychoanalysis*, 16, 397-416.

Barnett, J. (1980B), Self and character. *Journal of the American Academy of Psychoanalysis*, 8, 337-352.

Becker, E. (1973), *The Denial of Death*. New York: Free Press.

Bemporard, J., Smith, H., Hancon, G. Cicchetti, V. (1982), Borderline syndromes in childhood: Criteria for diagnosis. *American Journal of Psychiatry*, 139, 596-602.

Bender, L. (1934), Psychiatric mechanisms in child murderers. *Journal of Nervous & Mental Diseases*, 80, 32-47.

Bender, L. & Curan, F. (1940), Children and adolescents who kill. *Journal of Criminal Psychopathology*, 1, 297-322.

Bender, L. (1953), *Aggression, Hostility and Anxiety in Children.* Springfield: Charles C. Thomas.

Bender, L. (1959), Children and adolescents who have killed. *American Journal of Psychiatry,* 116, 510-513.

Bender, L. (1974), Aggression in children. In S. Frazier (Ed.) *Aggression.* Baltimore: Williams and Wilkins.

Berkowitz, D. Shapiro, R., Zinner, J. & Shapiro, E. (1974), Family contributions to narcissistic disturbances in adolescents. *International Review of Psychoanalysis,* 1, 353-367.

Bion, W. (1967), *Selected Thoughts: Selected Papers on Psychoanalysis.* New York: Aronson.

Blackman, N. Weiss, J., & Lamberts, J. (1963) The sudden murderer. *Archives of General Psychiatry,* 8, 289-294.

Bleiberg, E. (1987), Stages in the treatment of narcissistic children and adolescents. *Bulletin of the Menninger Clinic,* 51, 296-313.

Blos, P. (1962), *On Adolescence: A Psychoanalytic Interpretation.* Glencoe: Free Press.

Blos, P. (1966), The concept of acting out in relation to the adolescent process. In: E. Rexford (Ed.), *A Developmental Approach to Acting Out.* New York: International Universities Press, 1966.

Blos, P. (1967), The second individuation process of adolescence. *Psychoanalytic Study of the Child,* 22, 162-186.

Blos, P. (1968), Character formation in adolescence. *Psychoanalytic Study of the Child,* 23, 245-263.

Blos, P. (1971), Adolescent concretization: A contribution to the theory of delinquency. In: I. Marcus, (Ed.) *Currents in Psychoanalysis.* New York: International Universities Press.

Blos, P. (1972), The epigenesis of the adult neurosis. *Psychoanalytic Study of the Child,* 27, 106-135.

Blos, P. (1977), When and how does adolescence end: Structural criteria for adolescence closure. *Adolescent Psychiatry,* 5, 5-17.

Blos, P. (1979), *The Adolescent Passage: Developmental Issues.* New York: International Universities Press.

Blos, P. (1980), The life cycle as indicated by the nature of the transference in the psychoanalysis of adolescents. *International Journal of Psychoanalysis,* 61, 145-151.

Bonime, W. (1982), The paranoid and the depressive. *Contemporary Psychoanalysis,* 18, 556-574.

Bornstein, B. (1948), Emotional barriers in the understanding and treatment of children. *American Journal of Orthopsychiatry*, 18, 691-697.

Bowlby, J. (1953), *Child Care and the Growth of Love*. London: Hogarth Press.

Brandt, D. (1977), Separation and identity in adolescence: Erikson and Mahler-Some similarities. *Contemporary Psychoanalysis*, 13, 507-518.

Brenner, C. (1985), Countertransference as compromise formation. *Psychoanalytic Quarterly*, 54, 155-163.

Bromberg, P. (1983) The Mirror and the mask. On narcissism and psychoanalytic growth. *Contemporary Psychoanalysis*, 19, 359-381.

Bromberg, W. (1971), A psychological study of murderers. *International Journal of Psychoanalysis*, 32, 117-127.

Chavis, D. (1990), Intensive psychoanalytic psychotherapy of a severe narcissistic personality disorder in adolescence. *Adolescent Psychiatry*, 17, 109-128.

Chessick, R. (1992), The death instinct revisited. *Journal of the American Academy of Psychoanalysis*, 20, 3-18.

Chrzanowski, G. (1979), Participant observation and the working alliance. *Journal of the American Academy of Psychoanalysis*, 7, 259-269.

Compton, A. (1981), On the psychoanalytic theory of instinctual drives, IV: Instinctual drives and the ego-id-superego model. *Psychoanalytic Quarterly*, 50, 363-392.

Cooper, A. (1987), Changes in psychoanalytic ideas: Transference interpretation. *Journal of the American Psychoanalytic Association*: 35, 77-98.

Deutsch, F. (1957) A footnote to Freud's "Fragment of an analysis of a case of hysteria". In: *On the Mysterious Leap from the Mind to Body*. New York: International Universities Press.

Easson, W. & Steinhilber, R. (1961), Murderous Aggression by children and adolescents. *Archives of General Psychiatry*, 4, 1-9.

Eckstein, R. (1954), The space child's time machine: On reconstruction in the psychotherapeutic treatment of a schizophrenoid child. *American Journal of Orthopsychiatry*, 24, 492-506.

Eckstein, R. & Friedman, S. (1957), Acting out, play action and play acting. *Journal of the American Psychoanalytic Association*, 5, 581-629.

Eckstien, R. & Wallerstein, J. (1954), Observations on the psychology of borderline and psychotic children. *Psychoanalytic Study of the Child*, 9, 344-369.

Eckstein, R. & Wallerstein, J. (1957), Choice of interpretation in the treatment of borderline and psychotic children. *Bulletin of the Menninger Clinic*, 21, 199-208.

Egan, J. & Kernberg, P. (1984), Pathological narcissism in childhood. *Journal of the American Psychoanalytic Association*, 32, 39-63.

Eissler, K. (1950), Ego psychological implications of the psychoanalytic treatment of delinquents. *Psychoanalytic Study of the Child*, 5, 97-121.

Eissler, K. (1951), Remarks on the psychoanalysis of schizophrenia. *International Journal of Psychoanalysis*, 32, 1-18.

Epstein, L. & Feiner, A. (Eds.) (1979), *Countertransference: The Therapist's Contribution to Treatment*. New York: Aronson.

Erikson, E. (1950), *Childhood and Society*. New York: Norton.

Erikson, E. (1956), The problem of ego identity. *Journal of the American Psychoanalytic Association*, 4, 56-121.

Erikson, E. (1959A), *Identity and the Life Cycle*. New York: International Universities Press.

Erikson, E. (1959B), Late adolescence. In: E. Schlein (Ed.) *A Way of Looking at things: Selected Papers of Erik Erikson From 1930 - 1980*. New York: Norton: 1987.

Erikson, E. (1962), Reality and actuality. *Journal of the American Psychoanalytic Association*, 10, 451-474.

Erikson, E. (1968A), *Identity, Youth and Crisis*. New York: Norton.

Erikson, E. (1968B), Psychosocial Identity. In: E. Schlein (Ed.) *A Way of Looking at things: Selected Papers of Erik Erikson 1930- 1980*. New York: Norton, 1987.

Esman, A. (1980), Midadolescence - Foundations for later psychopathology. In: S. Greenspan & G. Pollack's (Eds.) *The Course of Life*. Washington, D.C.: NIMH.

Fairbairn, W. (1941), A revised psychopathology of the neuroses and the psychoses. *International Journal of Psychoanalysis*, 52, 250-277.

Fairbairn, W. (1943), The repression and the return of bad objects. In: *Psychoanalytic Studies of the Personality*. London: Tavistock,

1952.

Fairbairn, W. (1944), Endopsychic structure considered in terms of object relationships. *International Journal of Psychoanalysis*, 25, 70-73.

Fairbairn, W. (1952), *Psychoanalytic Studies of the Personality*, London: Tavistock.

Fairbairn, W. (1954), Observations on the nature of hysterical states. *British Journal of Medical Psychology*, 27, 105-125.

Fairbairn, W. (1963), Synopsis of an object relations theory of personality. *International Journal of Psychoanalysis*, 44, 224-225.

Federn, P. (1952), *Ego Psychology and the Psychoses*. New York: Basic Books.

Ferenczi, S. (1932), Confusion of tongues between adults and the child. In: *Final Contributions to Problems and Methods of Psychoanalysis*. New York: Brunner Mazel, 1980.

Fenichel, O. (1945), *The Psychoanalytic Theory of Neurosis*. New York: Norton.

Fenichel, O. (1953), The Psychoanalysis of character. In: *The Collected Papers of Otto Fenichel*. New York: Norton.

Finkelhor, D. (1984), *Child Sexual Abuse: New Theory and Research*. New York: Free Press.

Fintzy, R. (1971), Vicissitudes of the transitional object in a borderline child. *International Journal of Psychoanalysis*, 52, 107-114.

Fraiberg, S. (1969), Libido-object constancy and mental representation. *Psychoanalytic Study of the Child*, 24, 9-47.

Frankl, V. (1962), *Man's Search for Meaning*. Boston: Beacon.

Friedman, L. (1985), Toward a reconceptualization of guilt. *Contemporary Psychoanalysis*, 4, 501-548.

Freud, A. (1937), *The Ego and the Mechanisms of Defense*. New York: International Universities Press.

Freud, A. (1947), *The Psychoanalytic Treatment of Children*. London: Imago.

Freud, A. (1949), Certain types and stages of social maladjustment. In: *Introduction for Child Analysis and Other Papers*. New York: International Universities Press, 1969.

Freud, A. (1952), A connection between the states of negativism and emotional surrender. In: *Introduction for Child Analysis and Other Papers*. New York: International Universities Press, 1969.

Freud, A. (1958), Adolescence. *Psychoanalytic Study of the Child*, 13, 255-278.

Freud, A. (1965), *Normality and Pathology in Childhood*. New York: International Universities Press.

Freud, A. (1967), Comments on trauma. In: S. Furst (Ed.) *Psychic Trauma*. New York: International Universities Press.

Freud, A. (1968), Acting out. *International Journal of Psychoanalysis*, 49, 165-170.

Freud, A. (1980), Treatment Alliance. In: J. Sandler, H. Kennedy, & R. Tyson (Eds.) *The Technique of Child Psychoanalysis: Discussions with Anna Freud*. Cambridge: Harvard University Press.

Freud, S. (1905A), Three essays on the theory of sexuality. *The Standard Edition of the Complete Psychological Works of Sigmund Freud*, 7, 125-245, London: Hogarth Press.

Freud, S. (1905B), Fragment of analysis of a case of hysteria. *The Standard Edition of the Complete Psychological Works of Sigmund Freud*, 7, 1-122, London: Hogarth Press.

Freud, S. (1906), My views on the part played by sexuality in the etiology of the neuroses. *The Standard Edition of the Complete Psychological Works of Sigmund Freud*, 7, 269-279, London: Hogarth Press.

Freud, S. (1908), Character and anal eroticism. *The Standard Edition of the Complete Psychological Works of Sigmund Freud*. 9, 107-177, London: Hogarth Press.

Freud, S. (1911), Psychoanalytic notes on an autobiographical account of a case of paranoia. *The Standard Edition of the Complete Psychological Works of Sigmund Freud*. 12, 13-84. London: Hogarth Press.

Freud, S. (1912), The dynamics of transference. *The Standard Edition of the Complete Psychological Works of Sigmund Freud*. 12, 99-108, London: Hogarth Press.

Freud, S. (1914A), On narcissism: An introduction. *The Standard Edition of the Complete Psychological Works of Sigmund Freud*, 14, 67-102, London: Hogarth Press.

Freud, S. (1914B), Remembering, repeating & working through. *The Standard Edition of the Complete Psychological Works of Sigmund Freud*, 12, 147-156, London: Hogarth Press.

Freud, S. (1915), Repression. *The Standard Edition of the Complete*

Psychological Works of Sigmund Freud, 14, 141-159 London: Hogarth Press.

Freud, S. (1916), Introductory lectures on psychoanalysis. *The Standard Edition of the Complete Psychological Works of Sigmund Freud*, 14, 237-258 London: Hogarth Press.

Freud, S. (1920), Beyond the pleasure principle. *The Standard Edition of the Complete Psychological Works of Sigmund Freud*, 18, 3-64. London: Hogarth Press.

Freud, S. (1923), The ego and the id. *The Standard Edition of the Complete Psychological Works of Sigmund Freud*, 19, 11-66. London: Hogarth Press.

Freud, S. (1924), The economic problem of masochism. *The Standard Edition of the Complete Psychological Works of Sigmund Freud*, 20, 155-170, London: Hogarth Press.

Freud, S. (1926), Inhibitions, symptoms and anxiety. *The Standard Edition of the Complete Psychological Works of Sigmund Freud*, 20, 75-125, London: Hogarth Press.

Freud, S. (1930), Civilization and its discontents. *The Standard Edition of the Complete Psychological Works of Sigmund Freud*, 21, 59-145, London: Hogarth Press.

Freud, S. (1931), Libidinal types. *The Standard Edition of the Complete Psychological Works of Sigmund Freud*, 21, 215-220. London: Hogarth Press.

Freud, S. (1933), New introductory lectures on psychoanalysis. *The Standard Edition of the Complete Psychological Works of Sigmund Freud*, 22, 1-182, London: Hogarth Press.

Freud, S. (1937), Analysis terminable and interminable. *The Standard Edition of the Complete Psychological Works of Sigmund Freud*, 23, 216-253, London: Hogarth Press.

Freud, S. (1940), An outline of psychoanalysis. *The Standard Edition of the Complete Psychological Works of Sigmund Freud*, 23, 140-207, London: Hogarth Press.

Freud, S. (1950), Extracts from the Fliess papers. *The Standard Edition of the Complete Psychological Works of Sigmund Freud*, 1, 173-280, London: Hogarth Press.

Fromm, E. (1941), *Escape From Freedom*. New York: Holt, Rinehart and Winston.

Fromm, E. (1947), *Man For Himself*. New York: Holt, Rinehart and

Winston.

Fromm, E. (1951), *The Forgotten Language*. New York: Grove Press.

Fromm, E. (1973), *The Anatomy of Human Destructiveness*. New York: Holt, Rinehart and Winston.

Fromm-Reichmann, F. (1959), *Psychoanalysis and Psychotherapy*. D. Bullard. (Ed.) Chicago: University of Chicago Press.

Fromm-Reichmann, F. (1961), *Principles of Intensive Psychotherapy*. Chicago: University of Chicago Press.

Furman, E. (1956), An ego disturbance in a young child. *Psychoanalytic Study of the Child*, 11, 312-335.

Furst, S. (1967), *Psychic Trauma*. New York: Basic Books.

Gay, P. (1988), *Freud: A Life for Our Time*. New York: Norton.

Geleerd, E. (1961), Same aspects of ego vicissitudes in adolescence. *Journal of the American Psychoanalytic Association*, 9, 344-405.

Gesell, A. & Amatruda, C. (1941), *Developmental Diagnosis*. New York: Haeber.

Giovacchini, P. (1963), Integrative aspects of object relationships. *Psychoanalytic Quarterly*, 32, 393-407.

Giovacchini, P. (1972), Diagnostic and technical factors in treating the borderline adolescent. *International Journal of Child Psychotherapy*, 1, 47-64.

Giovacchini, P. (1979), *Treatment of Primitive Mental States*. New York: Aronson.

Giovacchini, P. (1984), *Countertransference: Triumphs and Catastrophes*. Northvale, N.J.: Aronson.

Giovacchini, P. (1985), The borderline adolescent as a transitional object: A common variation. *Adolescent Psychiatry*, 12, 233-250.

Glenn, J. (1980), Freud's adolescent patients: Katarina, Dora, and the "homosexual woman". In: Kanzer, M. & Glenn, J. (Eds.) *Freud and His Patients*. New York: Aronson.

Glover, E. (1956), *On the Early Development of the Mind*. New York: International Universities Press.

Glover, E. (1960), *The Roots of Crime*. New York: International Universities Press.

Goldberg, A. (1985), The definition and role of interpretation. In: *Progress in Self Psychology: Volume I*. New York: Guilford Press.

Green, A. (1981), Core affective disturbance in abused children. *Journal of the American Academy of Psychoanalysis*, 9, 435-446.

Greenacre, P. (1950), General problems of acting out. In: *Trauma, Growth and Personality*. New York: International Universities Press, 1952.

Greenacre, P. (1953), Certain relationships between fetishism and faulty development of the body image. *Psychoanalytic Study of the Child*, 8, 65-78.

Greenacre, P. (1958), Early physical determinants in the development of the sense of identity. *Journal of the American Psychoanalytic Association*, 6, 612-627.

Greenacre, P. (1967), The influence of infantile trauma on genetic patterns. In: *Emotional Growth*. New York: International Universities Press, 1971.

Greenacre, P. (1969), The fetish and the transitional object. *Psychoanalytic Study of the Child*, 24, 144-164.

Greenberg, J. and Mitchell, S. (1983), *Object Relations in Psychoanalytic Theory*. Cambridge: Harvard University Press.

Greenson, R. (1967), *The Technique and Practice of Psychoanalysis*. New York: International Universities Press.

Greenson, R. (1968), Disidentifying from mother. *International Journal of Psychoanalytis*, 49, 370-374.

Grunberger, B. (1971), *Narcissism: Psychoanalytic Essays*. New York: International Universities Press.

Guntrip, H. (1961), *Personality Structure and Human Interaction: The Developing Synthesis of Psychodynamic Theory*. London: Hogarth Press.

Guntrip, H. (1969), *Schizoid Phenomena, Object Relations and the Self*. London: Hogarth Press.

Guntrip, H. (1971), *Psychodynamic Theory, Therapy and the Self*. New York: Basic Books.

Guntrip, H. (1975), My experience of analysis with Fairbairn and Winnicott. *International Review of Psychoanalysis*, 2, 145-156.

Hamilton, N. (1988), *Self and Others: Object Relations Theory and Practice*. Northale, N.J.: Aronson.

Hamilton, N. (1989), A critical review of object relations theory. *American Journal of Psychiatry*, 146, 1552-1560.

Hartmann, H. (1950), Comments on the psychoanalytic theory of the ego. In: *Essays on Ego Psychology*. New York: International

Universities Press, 1964.

Hartmann, H. (1958), *Ego Psychology and the Problems of Adaptation.* New York: International Universities Press.

Hazell, J. (1991), Reflections on my experience of psychoanalysis with Guntrip. *Contemporary Psychoanalysis,* 27, 148-166.

Heiman, P. (1950), On countertransference. *International Journal of Psychoanalysis,* 31, 81-84.

Helfer, R. & Kempe, R. (1987), *The Battered Child.* Chicago: University of Chicago Press.

Herman, J., Perry, C., Van der Kolk, B. (1989), Childhood trauma in borderline personality disorder. *American Journal of Psychiatry,* 146, 490-495.

Hirsch, I. (1987), Varying models of analytic participation. *Journal of the American Academy of Psychoanalysis,* 15, 205-222.

Hirsch, I. & Aron, L. (1991), Participant observation, perspectivism, and countertransference. In: H. Seigal, L. Barbanel, I. Hirsch, J. Lasky, H. Silverman, and S. Warshaw (Eds.) *Pychoanalytic Reflections on Current Issues.* New York: New York University Press.

Horney, K. (1937), *The Neurotic Personality of Our Time.* New York: Norton.

Horney, K. (1939), *New Ways in Psychoanalysis.* New York: Norton.

Horney, K. (1945), *Our Inner Conflicts.* New York: International Universities Press.

Horney, K. (1951), *Neurosis and Human Growth.* New York: Norton.

Hughes, L. (1989), *Reshaping the Psychoanalytic Domain.* Berkeley: University of California Press.

Hurvich, M. Annihilation anxiety: An introduction. In: *Psychoanalytic Reflections on Current Issues.* H. Siegel, L. Barbanel, I. Hirsch, J. Lasky, H. Siverman & S. Warshaw (Eds.) New York: New York University Press, 1991.

Jacobson, E. (1961), Adolescent moods and the remodeling of psychic structures in adolescence. *The Psychoanalytic Study of the Child,* 16, 164-183.

Jacobson, E. (1964), *The Self and the Object World.* New York: International Universities Press.

Johnson, A. & Szurek, S. (1952), The genesis of antisocial acting out in children and adults. *Psychoanalytic Quarterly,* 21, 323-343.

Jones, E. (1922), Some problems of adolescence. In: *Papers on Psychoanalysis*. London: Balliere, Tindall, & Cox, 1948.

Jones, E. (1929), The psychopathology of anxiety. In: *Papers on Psychoanalysis*. London: Balliere, Tindall, & Cox, 1948.

Josselson, R. (1980), Ego development in adolescence. In: J. Adelson (Ed.) *Handbook of Adolescent Psychology*. New York: Wiley.

Josselson, R. (1987), Identity diffusion: A long term follow up. *Adolescent Psychiatry*, 14, 230-258.

Kanzer, M. (1957), Acting out, sublimation and reality testing. *Journal of the American Psychoanalytic Association*, 5, 663-684.

Kanzer, M. (1980), Dora's imagery: The flight from a burning house. In: Kanzer, M. & Glenn, J. (Eds.) *Freud and His Patients*. New York: Aronson.

Kennedy, H. (1986), Trauma in childhood. *The Psychoanalytic Study of the Child*, 41, 209-219.

Kernberg, O. (1967), Borderline personality organization. *Journal of the American Psychoanalytic Association*, 15, 641-685.

Kernberg, O. (1968), The treatment of patients with borderline personality organization. *International Journal of Psychoanalysis*, 49, 600-619.

Kernberg, O. (1975), *Borderline Conditions and Pathological Narcissism*. New York: Aronson.

Kernberg, O. (1976), *Object Relations Theory and Clinical Psychoanalysis*. New York: Aronson.

Kernberg, O. (1979), Psychoanalytic psychotherapy with borderline adolescents. *Adolescent Psychiatry*, 7, 294-321.

Kernberg, P. (1979) Psychoanalytic profile of the borderline adolescent. *Adolescent Psychiatry*, 7, 234-250.

Kernberg, P. (1980), Childhood Psychosis: A psychoanalytic perspective. In: S. Greenspan, & G. Pollack (Eds.) *The Course of Life Volume I: Infancy and early childhood*. Washington, D.C. NIMH.

Kernberg, P. (1982), Update of borderline disorders in children. *Journal of the National Association of Private Psychiatric Hospitals*, 13, 4-12.

Khan, M. (1963), Ego ideal, excitement, and the threat of annihilation. *Journal of Hillside Hospital*, 12, 195-217.

Khan, M. (1969), On symbiotic omnipotence. In: *The Privacy of the Self*. New York: International Universities Press, 1974.

Khan, M. (1972), Dread of surrender to resourceless dependence in the psychoanalytic situation. In: *The Privacy of the Self*. New York: International Universities Press.

Khan, M. (1974), Silence as communication. In: *The Privacy of the Self*. New York: International Universities Press.

Khan, M. (1979), *Alienation in Perversions*. New York: International Universities Press.

Khan, M. (1986), Outrageousness, compliance and authenticity. *Contemporary Psychoanalysis*, 22, 629-650.

Khan, M. (1989), *The Long Wait and Other Psychoanalytic Narratives*. New York: Summit Books.

Klein, M. (1923), Early analysis. In: *Love, Guilt, and Reparation and Other Works*, 1921-1945. London: Hogarth Press, 1975.

Klein, M. (1928), Early stages of the Oedipus complex. In: *Love, Guilt, and Reparation and Other Works*, 1921-1945. London: Hogarth Press, 1975.

Klein, M. (1932), *The Psychoanalysis of Children*. London: Hogarth Press.

Klein, M. (1935), A contribution to the psychoanalysis of manic depressive states. In: *Contributions to Psychoanalysis, 1921-1945*. New York: McGraw Hill, 1964.

Klein, M. (1946), Notes on some schizoid mechanisms. In: *Envy, Gratitude, and Other Works*, 1946-1963, New York: Delacorte Press, 1975.

Klein, M. (1948), On the theory of anxiety and guilt. In: *Envy, Gratitude, and Other Works*, 1946-1963, New York: Delacorte Press, 1975.

Klein, M. (1958), On the development of mental functioning. *International Journal of Psychoanalysis*, 39, 84-90.

Klein, M. (1959), Our adult world and its roots in infancy. In: *Envy, Gratitude and Other Works, 1946-1963*. New York: Delacrote Press, 1975.

Klein, M. (1961), *Narrative of Child Analysis*. London: Hogarth Press.

Klein, M. (1964), *Contributions to Psychoanalysis: 1921-1945*. London: Hogarth Press.

Klein, M. (1975), *Envy, Gratitude, and Other Works, 1946-1963*. New York: Delacorte Press.

Kohut, H. (1966), Forms and transformations of narcissism. *Journal of the American Psychoanalytic Association*, 14, 243-272.

Kohut, H. (1968), The psychoanalytic treatment of narcissistic personality disorders. *Psychoanalytic Study of the Child*, 1975, 23, 86-113.

Kohut, H. (1971), *The Analysis of the Self*. New York: International Universities Press.

Kohut, H. (1972), Thoughts on narcissism and narcissistic rage. *Psychoanalytic Study of the Child*, 27, 360-399.

Kohut, H. (1977), *The Restoration of the Self*. New York: International Universities Press.

Kohut H. & Wolf, E. (1978), The disorders of the self and their treatment: An outline. *International Journal of Psychoanalysis*, 59, 413-425.

Krystall, H. (1978), Trauma and affects. *Psychoanalytic Study of the Child*, 36, 81-116.

Kwawer, J. (1981), Object relations and interpersonal theories. *Contemporary Psychoanalysis*, 17, 276-289.

Laing, R. (1960), *The Divided Self*, London: Tavistock Publications.

Laing, R. (1970), *Knots*. New York: Random House.

Landis, B. (1981), Discussions with Harry Guntrip. *Contemporary Psychoanalysis*, 17, 112-117.

Laufer, M. (1968), The body image, the function of masturbation and adolescence: Problems of the ownership of the body. *Psychoanalytic Study of the Child*, 23, 114-137.

Laufer, M. (1976), The central masturbation fantasy, the final sexual organization and adolescence. *Psychoanalytic Study of the Child*, 31, 297-316.

Laufer, M. (1978), The nature of adolescent patterning and the psychoanalytic process. *Psychoanalytic Study of the Child*, 33, 307-322. Laufer, M. (1981), Adolescent breakdown and the transference neurosis. *International Journal of Psychoanalysis*, 62, 51-59.

Laufer, M. & Laufer, E. (1984), *Adolescence and Developmental Breakdown*. New Haven: Yale University Press.

Lax, R. (Ed.), (1989), *Essential Papers on Character Neurosis and Treatment*. New York: New York University Press.

Lefer, L. (1984), The fine edge of violence. *Journal of the American Academy of Psychoanalysis*, 12, 253-268.

Levenson, E. (1981), Facts or fantasies. On the nature of psychoanalytic data. *Contemporary Psychoanalysis*, 17, 486-500.

Lewis, D. (1983), Neuropsychiatric vulnerabilities and violence in juvenile delinquency. *Psychiatric Clinics of North America*, 4, 707-714.

Lewis, D., May, E., Jackson, L., Aaronson, R., Restifo, M., Serra, S., & Sinos, A. (1985) Biopsychosocial characteristics of children who later murder. *American Journal of Psychiatry*, 143, 1151-1167.

Little, M. (1951), Countertransference and the patient's response to it. *International Journal of Psychoanalysis*, 32, 32-40.

Little, M. (1957), "R". The analyst's total response to his patient's needs. *International Journal of Psychoanalysis*, 38, 240-254.

Little, M. (1965), Transference in borderline states. *International Journal of Psychoanalysis*, 47, 476-485.

Little, M. (1981), *Transference Neurosis and Transference Psychosis*. New York: Aronson.

Little, M. (1990), *Psychotic Anxieties and Containment*. Northvale, N.J.: Aronson.

London, L. (1931), *The Call of the Wild*. New York: MacMillan.

Mahler, M. (1958), On the crucial phases of integration of the sense of identity: Separation-Individuation and Bisexual Identity. *Journal of the American Psychoanalytic Association*, 6, 612-627.

Mahler, M. (1967), *On Human Symbiosis and the Vicissitudes of Individuation*. New York: International Universities Press.

Mahler, M. (1971), A study of the separation-individuation process and its possible application to borderline phenomena in the psychoanalytic situation. *Psychoanalytic Study of the Child*, 26, 403-424.

Mahler, M. Pine, F. & Bergman, A. (1975), *The Psychological Birth of the Human Infant*. New York: Basic Books.

Mahron, R. (1981), The negative transference in the treatment of juvenile delinquents. *Annual of Psychoanalysis*, 9, 21-42.

Mahron, R. (1990), Violence and unrestrained behavior in adolescents. *Adolescent Psychiatry*, 17, 419-432.

Marcus, S. (1974) Freud and Dora. In: *Representations: Essays on Literature and Society*. New York: Random House, 1976.

Margolis, M. (1984), A case of mother adolescent son incest. A follow up study. *Psychoanalytic Quarterly*, 53, 355-385.

Marshall, R. (1972), The treatment of resistance of children and adolescents to psychotherapy. *Psychotherapy, Theory, Practice and Research*, 1, 143-148.

Marshall, R. (1979), Countertransference in the psychotherapy of children and adolescents, *Contemporary Psychoanalysis*, 15, 595-629.

Masterson, J. (1967), *The Psychiatric Dilemma of Adolescence: A Developmental approach*. Boston: Little Brown. New York: John Wiley & Sons.

Masterson, J. (1972), *The Borderline Adolescent: A Developmental Approach*. New York: John Wiley & Sons.

Masterson, J. (1974), Intensive psychotherapy of the adolescent with a borderline syndrome. In: S. Arieti (Ed.), *American Handbook of Psychiatry. Volume 2*. New York: Basic Books.

Masterson, J. & Rinsley, D. (1975), The borderline syndrome: the role of the mother in the genesis and structure of the borderline personality. *International Journal of Psychoanalysis*, 56, 163-177.

McCarthy, J. (1980), *Death Anxiety: The Loss of the Self*. New York: Gardner Press, John Wiley & Sons.

Meissner, W. (1978), *The Paranoid Process*. New York: Aronson.

Meloy, J. (1988), Violent and homicidal behavior in primitive mental states. *Journal of the American Academy of Psychoanalysis*, 15, 381-394.

Menninger, K. & Mayman, M. (1956), Episodic dyscontrol: A third order of stress adaption. *Bulletin of the Mennenger Clinic*, 20, 153.

Miller, J. (1985), How Kohut actually worked. In: *Progress in Self Psychology. Volume I*. New York: Guilford Press.

Miller, O. & Looney, J. (1974), The prediction of adolescent homicide: Episodic dyscontrol and dehumanization. *American Journal of Psychoanalysis*. 34, 187-198

Mitchell, S. (1988), *Relational Concepts in Psychoanalysis*. Cambridge: Harvard University Press.

Mittelman, B. (1954), Motility in infants, children and adults, patterning and psychodynamics. *Psychoanalytic Study of the Child*, 9, 142-177.

Mittelman, B. (1955), Motor patterns and genital behavior: fetishism.

Psychoanalytic Study of the Child, 10, 241-263.

Modell, A. (1968), *Object Love and Reality: An Introduction to a Psychoanalytic Theory of Object Relations.* New York: International Universities Press.

Muslin, H. & Gill, M. (1978), Transference in the Dora case. *Journal of the American Psychoanalytic Association,* 36, 311-328.

Obrien, J. (1987), The effects of incest on female adolescent development. *Journal of the American Academy of Psychoanalysis,* 15, 83-92.

Ornstein, P. (1978), (Ed.), *The Search for the Self - Selected Writings of Heinz Kohut, 1955-1970.* New York: International Universities Press.

Perry, H. (1982), *Psychiatrist of America. The Life of Harry Stack Sullivan.* Cambridge: Harvard University Press.

Pine, F. (1974), On the concept "borderline" in children. *Psychoanalytic Study of the Child,* 29, 341-368.

Pine, F. (1985), *Developmental Theory and Clinical Process.* New Haven: Yale University Press.

Racker, H. (1968), *Transference and Countertransference.* New York: International Universities Press.

Redl, F. (1951), *Children Who Hate.* New York: MacMillan.

Reich, A. (1960), Pathologic forms of self esteem regulation. *Journal of the American Psychoanalytic Association,* 15, 215-232.

Reich, A. (1973), *Psychoanalytic Contributions.* New York: International Universities Press.

Reich, W. (1933) *Character Analysis.* New York: Simon and Schuster.

Reichard, S., & Tillman, C. (1950), Murder and suicide as defenses against schizophrenic psychosis. *Journal of Clinical Psychopathology,* 11, 149.

Reiner, B. & Kaufman, I. (1959), Character disorders. In: *Parents of Delinquents.* New York: Family Service Association of America.

Rheingold, J. (1967), *The Mother, Anxiety and Death.* Boston: Little Brown.

Rinsley, D. (1978), Borderline psychopathology. A review of aetiology, dynamics, and treatment. *International Review of Psychoanalysis,* 5, 45-54.

Rinsley, D. (1980), Diagnosis and treatment of borderline and narcissistic children and adolescents. *Bulletin of the Menninger Clinic,* 44,

147-170.

Ritvo, S. (1971), Late Adolescence. *Psychoanalytic Study of the Child*, 26, 241-263.

Rogow, W. (1978), A further footnote to Freud's "Fragment of an analysis of a case of hysteria". *Journal of the American Psychoanalytic Association*, 29, 331-376.

Rosen, J. (1953), *Direct Analysis: Selected Papers*. New York: Grune & Stratton.

Rosenfeld, H. (1952), Transference phenomena and transference analysis in an acute schizophrenic patient. *International Journal of Psychoanalysis*, 33, 457-464.

Rothstein, A. (1984), The fear of humiliation. *Journal of the American Psychoanalytic Association*, 32, 99-116.

Sandler, J. (1981), Character traits and object relationships. *Psychoanalytic Quarterly*, 50, 694-708.

Sargent, D. (1965), Children who kill. A family conspiracy. *Social Work*, 13, 35-42.

Schachtel, E. (1959), *Metamorphosis*. New York: Basic Books.

Schilder, P. (1935), *The Image and Appearance of the Human Body*. New York: International Universities Press.

Schimel, J. (1992), The role of humor as an integrating factor in adolescent development. *Adolescent Psychiatry*, 18, 118-126.

Schowalter, J. (1985), Countertransference in work with children. Review of a neglected concept. *Journal of the American Academy of Child Psychiatry*, 25, 40-45.

Searles, H. (1961A), Schizophrenia and the inevitability of death. *Psychiatric Quarterly*, 35, 631-635.

Searles, H. (1961B), Phases of patient therapist interaction in the psychotherapy of chronic schizophrenia. *British Journal of Medical Psychology*, 34, 161-192.

Searles, H. (1965), *Collected Papers on Schizophrenia and Related Subjects*. New York: International Universities Press.

Searles, H. (1977), Dual and multiple identity processes in borderline individual and its effect upon the sense of personal identity. In: *My Work with Borderline Patients*. New York: Aronson, 1986.

Searles, H. (1978), Non differentiation of ego functioning in the borderline individual and its effect upon the sense of personal identity. In: *My Work with Borderline Patients*. New York:

Aronson, 1986.

Searles, H. (1979), *Countertransference and Related Subjects - Selected Papers*. New York: International Universities Press.

Searles, H. (1986), *My Work with Borderline Patients*. New York: Aronson.

Segal, H. (1964), *An Introduction to the Work of Melanie Klein*. London: Heinemann.

Segal, H. (1983), Some clinical interpretations of Melanie Klein's work. *International Journal of Psychoanalysis*, 64, 269-275.

Settlage, C. (1977), The psychoanalytic understanding of narcissistic and borderline personality disorders. *Journal of the American Psychoanalytic Association*, 25, 805-833.

Shapiro, D. (1965), *Neurotic Styles*. New York: Basic Books.

Shapiro, E. & Freedman, J. (1985), Family dynamics of adolescent suicide. *Adolescent Psychiatry*, 14, 191-207.Shapiro, E., Zinner,

Shapiro, J., R. Zinner, J., Shapiro, R., & Berkowitz, D. (1975), The influence of family experience on borderline personality development. *International Review of Psychoanalysis*, 2, 399-411.

Sharpe, E. (1950), *Collected Papers on Psychoanalysis*. London: Hogarth Press.

Shatan, C. (1977), Bogus manhood, bogus honor: Surrender, and transfiguration in the United States Marine Corps. *Psychoanalytic Review*, 64, 585-610.

Shengold, L. (1989), *Soul Murder*. New Haven: Yale University Press.

Singer, E. (1965), *Key Concepts in Psychotherapy*. New York: Basic Books.

Singer, E. (1971), The patient aids the analyst: Some clinical and theoretical observations. In: B. Landis & E. Tauber (Eds). *In the Name of Life, Essays in Honor of Erik Fromm*. New York: Holt, Rinehart and Winston.

Slipp, S. (1977), Interpersonal factors in hysteria. *Journal of the American Academy of Psychoanalysis*, 5, 359-376.

Smith, S. (1965), The adolescent murderer. *Archives of General Psychiatry*, 13, 310-319

Spiegel, R. (1972), A violent youth gang, their dreams and life situations, In: *Psychoanalytic Perspectives on Aggression*. Garden City: Adelphi University Press.

Spiegel, R. (1977), Freud and the women in his world. *Journal of the*

American Academy of Psychoanalysis, 5, 377-402.

Spotnitz, H. (1969), *Modern Psychoanalysis With the Schizophrenic Patient*. New York: Grune and Stratton.

Spruriell, V. (1975), Narcissistic transformations in adolescence. *International Journal of Psychoanalytic Psychotherapy*, 4, 518-536.

Stern, M. (1968A), The fear of death and neurosis. *Journal of the American Psychoanalytic Association*, 13, 16-31.

Stern, M. (1968B), Death and trauma. *International Journal of Psychoanalysis*, 52, 277-288.

Stolorow, R. (1975), The narcissistic functions of masochism and sadism. *International Journal of Psychoanalysis*, 56, 441-448.

Stone, M. (1990), *The Fate of Borderline Patients*. New York: Guilford.

Sugar, M. (1979), Therapeutic approaches to the borderline adolescent. *Adolescent Psychiatry*, 7, 343-361.

Sugar, M. (1990), Developmental anxieties of adolescence. *Adolescent Psychiatry*, 17, 385-403.

Sullivan, H. (1940), *Conceptions of Modern Psychiatry*. New York: Norton.

Sullivan, H. (1953), *The Interpersonal Theory of Psychiatry*. New York: Norton.

Sullivan, H. (1954), *The Psychiatric Interview*. New York: Norton.

Sullivan, H. (1956), *Clinical Studies in Psychiatry*. New York: Norton.

Sutherland, J. (1989), *Fairbairn's Journey Into the Interior*. London: Free Association Books.

Terr, L. (1988), What happens to the memories of childhood trauma? *Journal of the American Academy of Child and Adolescent Psychiatry*, 27, 96-104.

Thompson, C. (1978), Sullivan and psychoanalysis. *Contemporary Psychoanalysis*, 14, 488-501.

Ticho, E. (1978), Harry Stack Sullivan and object relations. *Psychiatry*, 41, 141-150.

Toch, H. (1969), *An Inquiry Into the Psychology of Violence*. Chicago: Aldine Press.

Tylim, I. (1978), Narcissistic transference and countertransference in adolescent treatment. *Psychoanalytic Study of the Child*, 32, 279-292.

Westen, D., Ludolph, P., Silk, K., Kellom, A., Gold, L., & Lohr, M.

(1990), Object relations in borderline adolescents and adults: Developmental differences. *Adolescent Psychiatry*, 17, 360-384.

Winn, D. (1975), Adolescents who killed. Unpublished paper.

Winnicott, D. (1945), Primitive emotional development. In: *Through Paediatrics to Psychoanalysis: Collected Papers*. London: Hogarth Press, 1975.

Winnicott, D. (1947), Hate in the countertransference. In: *Through Paediatrics to Psychoanalysis: Collected Papers*. London: Hogarth Press, 1975.

Winnicott, D. (1951), Transitional objects and transitional phenomena. In: *Through Paediatrics to Psychoanalysis: Collected Papers*. London: Hogarth Press, 1975.

Winnicott, D. (1954A), Metapsychological and clinical aspects of regression within the psychoanalytic setup. In: *Through Paediatrics to Psychoanalysis: Collected Papers*. London: Hogarth Press, 1975.

Winnicott, D. (1954B), Withdrawal and regression. In: *Through Paediatrics to Psychoanalysis: Collected Papers*. London: Hogarth Press, 1975.

Winnicott, D. (1956A), Primary maternal preoccupation. In: *Through Paediatrics to Psychoanalysis: Collected Papers*. London: Hogarth Press, 1975.

Winnicott, D. (1956B), Clinical varieties of transference. In: *Through Paediatrics to Psychoanalysis: Collected Papers*. London: Hogarth Press, 1975.

Winnicott, D. (1958), The capacity to be alone. In: *The Maturational Processes and the Facilitating Environment*. London: Hogarth Press, 1965.

Winnicott, D. (1961), Adolescence. In: *The Family and Individual Development*. London: Tavistock Publications, 1965.

Winnicott, D. (1962), Ego integration in child development. In: *The Maturational Processes and the Facilitating Environment*. London: Hogarth Press, 1965.

Winnicott, D. (1965A), *The Maturational Processes and the Facilitating Environment*. London: Hogarth Press, 1965.

Winnicott, D. (1965B), Adolescence: Struggling through the doldrums. In: *The Family and Individual Development*. London: Tavistock Publications, 1965.

Winnicott, E. (1968), Adolescent immaturity. In: C. Winnicott, R. Shepherd, & M. Davis (Eds.) *Home Is Where We Start From: Essays by a Psychoanalyst.* New York: Norton, 1986.

Winnicott, D. (1971), The concept of trauma in relation to the development of the individual within the family. In: *Playing and Reality.* New York: Basic Books.

Winnicott, D. (1971), *Therapeutic Consultations in Child Psychiatry.* London: Hogarth Press.

Winnicott, D. (1974), Fear of breakdown. *International Review of Psychoanalysis*, 1, 103-107.

Winnicott, D. (1986A), Adolescent Immaturity. In: C. Winnicott, R. Shepherd, & M. Davis (Eds). *Home Is Where We Start From: Essays by a Psychoanalyst.* New York: Norton.

Winnicott, D. (1986B), *Holding and Interpretation. Fragment of an Analysis.* London: Hogarth Press.

Winnicott, D. (1987), F. Rodman (Ed.) *The Spontaneous Gesture: Selected Letters of Donald Winnicott.* Cambridge: Harvard University Press.

Winnicott, D. (1988), *Human Nature.* New York: Schocken Books.

Winnicott, D. (1989), Deductions drawn from a psychotherapeutic interview with an adolescent. In: C. Winnicott, R. Shepherd, & M. Davis (Eds.) *Psychoanalytic Explorations.* Cambridge: Harvard University Press.

Wolstein, B. (1975), Countertransference: The psychoanalyst's shared experience and inquiry with his patient. *Journal of the American Academy of Psychoanalysis*, 13, 77-89.

Wolstein, B. (1988) (Ed.) *Essential Papers on Countertransference.* New York: New York University Press.

Wolf, E. (1982), Adolescence: Psychology of the self and self objects. *Adolescent Psychiatry*, 12, 171-181.

INDEX

About the Author

James B. McCarthy, Ph.D. is a psychoanalyst in private practice in Forest Hills and Manhattan, New York who completed his training at the New York University Postdoctoral Program in Psychotherapy and Psychoanalysis. His current affiliations are: Director of Psychology, Queens Children's Psychiatric Center, Faculty, Manhattan Institute for Psychoanalysis, Clinical Professor of Psychology, St. John's University and Supervisory Faculty, New York University and Yeshiva University Doctoral Programs. Previously he was Attending Psychologist, Lenox Hill Hospital, and on the Faculty of New York Medical College. Dr. McCarthy is also the author of *Death Anxiety: the Loss of the Self* (1980) and numerous papers on developmental issues in psychoanalysis.